ROUTLEDGE LIBRARY EDITIONS: 17TH CENTURY PHILOSOPHY

Volume 8

LEIBNIZ' DOCTRINE OF NECESSARY TRUTH

LEIBNIZ' DOCTRINE OF NECESSARY TRUTH

MARGARET DAULER WILSON

LONDON AND NEW YORK

First published in 1990 by Garland

This edition first published in 2020
by Routledge
2 Park Square, Milton Park, Abingdon, Oxon OX14 4RN

and by Routledge
52 Vanderbilt Avenue, New York, NY 10017

Routledge is an imprint of the Taylor & Francis Group, an informa business

© 1990 Margaret Dauler Wilson

All rights reserved. No part of this book may be reprinted or reproduced or utilised in any form or by any electronic, mechanical, or other means, now known or hereafter invented, including photocopying and recording, or in any information storage or retrieval system, without permission in writing from the publishers.

Trademark notice: Product or corporate names may be trademarks or registered trademarks, and are used only for identification and explanation without intent to infringe.

British Library Cataloguing in Publication Data
A catalogue record for this book is available from the British Library

ISBN: 978-0-367-27875-5 (Set)
ISBN: 978-0-429-29844-8 (Set) (ebk)
ISBN: 978-0-367-33462-8 (Volume 8) (hbk)
ISBN: 978-0-367-33464-2 (Volume 8) (pbk)
ISBN: 978-0-429-31995-2 (Volume 8) (ebk)

Publisher's Note
The publisher has gone to great lengths to ensure the quality of this reprint but points out that some imperfections in the original copies may be apparent.

Disclaimer
The publisher has made every effort to trace copyright holders and would welcome correspondence from those they have been unable to trace.

Leibniz' Doctrine of Necessary Truth

Margaret Dauler Wilson

GARLAND PUBLISHING
NEW YORK & LONDON
1990

Copyright © 1990 by
Margaret Dauler Wilson
All Rights Reserved

Library of Congress Cataloging-in-Publication Data

Wilson, Margaret Dauler, 1939–.
Leibniz' doctrine of necessary truth/ Margaret Dauler Wilson
p. cm. — (Harvard dissertations in philosophy)
Thesis (Ph. D.)—Harvard University, 1965.
Includes bibliographical references.
ISBN 0-8240-3767-7
1. Leibniz, Gottfried Wilhelm, 1646–1716—Contributions to doctrine of necessary truth. 2. Necessity (Philosophy) 3. Truth. I. Title.
B2599.T78W54   1990
121'.092—dc20   89-49439

All volumes printed on acid-free, 250-year-life paper
Manufactured in the United States of America

Design by Julie Threlkeld

PREFACE TO THE GARLAND EDITION

I first became interested in the topic of this dissertation in the early 1960's; the work was completed in 1965. At that time very little serious work was being done in English on Leibniz, or indeed on early modern philosophy generally. But since the late sixties there has been, of course, a tremendous output of excellent writing on this period, and an intensification of interest that is virtually world-wide. It would be impossible to indicate the bearing of all this important work on the topics explored in the thesis. Particularly notable in this connection, however, is the range of recent work on the Leibniz-Locke relation (the main subject of Chapter II), and on Leibniz's theory (or theories) of contingency (which I touch on briefly in the Conclusion). Developments in metaphysics, philosophy of language, philosophical logic, and epistemology during the last twenty-five years are also relevant to the topics covered here. For instance, a certain anti-realist complacency which the reader may detect in Chapter IV would today have to confront the strong "neo-Aristotelian" currents prevalent since the early seventies. My total disregard of the "true in all possible worlds" analysis of necessary truth would require either defense or remedy today, in view of the tremendous emphasis on this analysis in recent metaphysics and modal semantics, and the related interest in the role of possible worlds theory in Leibniz' philosophy. (My neglect of this analysis was due to the fact that Leibniz seldom, if ever, relies on possible worlds theory in his explicit accounts of (absolutely) necessary truth. This consideration has, however, weighed less heavily with some later commentators: see, for instance, Benson Mates, *The Philosophy of Leibniz* (Oxford University Press, 1986), 107ff.)

Naturally I feel somewhat diffident about having the thesis published, when there has been so much change of intellectual climate since the time it was submitted. However, a fair amount of the material it embodies still strikes me as worthwhile--even reasonably fresh--and I hope it may still be of use to others.

Two previous publications were derived from the thesis: "Leibniz and Locke on First Truths" (*Journal of the History of Ideas*, vol. 68, July, 1967); and "On Leibniz's Explication of 'Necessary Truth'," (*Studia Leibnitiana*, Supplement, vol. III, 1969; reprinted in H. Frankfurt, editor, *Leibniz: A Collection of Critical Essays*, Doubleday, 1972). These papers include some minor revisions of the thesis argument. I have not attempted to incorporate these, or any other, changes of substance into the present edition. A complete retyping has, however, permitted the correction of typographical errors and occasional adjustments in punctuation. (For practical reasons I decided against trying to correct one pervasive anomaly in the original punctuation: the failure to use single, rather than double, quotation marks to indicate the "mentioning" of a term.)

I want to thank Helaine Randerson for the retyping, and my husband Emmett for again typing the Greek. I would like to dedicate this edition to the memory of my mother, Margaret Hodge Dauler McPherson, who died this year.

MDW

Princeton, NJ
August, 1989

ACKNOWLEDGMENTS

Chief credit for whatever may be of value in this essay must go to my advisor, Professor Morton White, through whose course on the A Priori I was first introduced to the critical study of historical doctrines of necessary truth, and who has provided encouragement, stimulation, and indispensable criticism and suggestions at every stage of the development of the thesis. Next I wish to express my gratitude to the second member of my thesis committee, Professor Burton Dreben, both for many valuable suggestions concerning the thesis itself, and for the great benefits of his insight into contemporary controversies concerning the concept of necessity and the foundations of mathematics. I also owe thanks to Mrs. Martha Kneale of Lady Margaret Hall, Oxford, and to Professor Willis Doney of Dartmouth, from whose detailed knowledge of the philosophy of Leibniz and of the Leibniz literature I have profited immensely, and who have given me very kind encouragement and advice at different stages of my work. I must further acknowledge specific debts to Professor James J. Walsh of Columbia and Professor B.J. Diggs of Illinois, both of whom assisted my investigation of Leibniz' medieval forebearers with fruitful suggestions; and to my husband, Emmett Wilson, for helpful references to the works of Descartes and his commentators.

Finally, I wish to thank Radcliffe College; The Committee on General Scholarships and the Sheldon Fund of Harvard University; and Vassar College for fellowships and financial assistance which greatly facilitated the completion of this work.

TABLE OF CONTENTS

PREFACE TO THE GARLAND EDITION	i
ACKNOWLEDGMENTS	iii
ABBREVIATIONS	vi
INTRODUCTION	1
CHAPTER I: LEIBNIZ' DOCTRINE AND SOME HISTORICAL ANTECEDENTS	5
CHAPTER II: SEVENTEENTH CENTURY OPPOSITION: THE INTUITIONISM OF DESCARTES AND LOCKE	43
CHAPTER III: SOME CRITICAL CHALLENGES TO LEIBNIZ' DOCTRINE OF NECESSITY	80
CHAPTER IV: LEIBNIZ' OPPOSITION TO CONVENTIONALISM AND HIS CONCEPTION OF DEFINITION	109
CONCLUSION	131
BIBLIOGRAPHY	136

ABBREVIATIONS

G.   *Die philosophischen Schriften von G.W. Leibniz*, ed. G.J. Gerhardt (Berlin: Weidmannsche Buchhandlung, 1875-90).

Log.   Louis Couturat: *La logique de Leibniz d'apres des Documents inédits* (Hildesheim: George Olms, 1961)

N.E.   *Nouveaux essais* in *Gottfried Wilhelm Leibniz: Sämtliche Schriften und Briefe*, ed. Deutschen Akademie der Wissenschaften, Reihe VI, BD. VI (Berlin: Akademie-Verlag, 1962).

O.F.   *Opuscules et fragments inédits de Leibniz*, ed. Louis Couturat (Hildesheim: George Olms, 1961).

S.   *G.W. Leibniz: Opuscula Philosophica Selecta*, ed. Paul Schrecker (Paris: Librairie Philosophique J. Vrin, 1959).

T.   *Leibniz: Essais de théodicée sur la bonté de Dieu la liberté de l'homme et l'origine du mal*, suivi de *La monadologie*, ed. Jacques Jalabert (Aubier: Editions Montaigne, 1962).

INTRODUCTION

Although the basic tenet of Leibniz' doctrine of necessity--that necessary truths are those derivable from the principle of identity by the substitution of definitions--is well known, no systematic study of this historically and philosophically important doctrine has yet appeared. In attempting to provide such a study, I have chosen to concentrate on four main issues, examination of which seems to me most helpful in the effort to gain an understanding of the nature, significance, and difficulties of Leibniz' position on this subject.

Expositors of Leibniz' philosophy sometimes characterize his definition of necessity as "traditional."[1] I shall therefore begin by considering views on the concept of necessity advanced by certain of his philosophic predecessors which in fact anticipate in various ways his own position. The aim of this chapter will be to indicate the extent to which Leibniz' doctrine does incorporate or reflect established tradition, and the extent to which it involves original developments. It will be found that Leibniz' definition actually represents the synthesis of *two* traditions--that of Aristotle and the Scholastics on the one hand, and of the geometers and Hobbes on the other hand. From the former derive the conception of the principle of identity as the first principle of knowledge, and the view that "impossible" may be equated with "self-contradictory"; from the latter comes emphasis on proof by reduction to primitives, and on the role of definition in demonstration.

I shall then go on to examine the conflict between Leibniz' reductionistic and formalistic views (i.e. his preoccupation with the problem of formal proof) and the opposing intuitionism and anti-reductionism of his seventeenth century contemporaries, Descartes and Locke. Besides trying to clarify the basis and nature of this conflict, I shall maintain that Locke's detailed arguments in the *Essay* against the validity of the enterprise of reduction are not effective against Leibniz' position (although at the same time Leibniz' replies to Locke in the *Nouveaux essais* are in some respects unsatisfactory). In the course of this discussion it will be necessary to evaluate the significance, for Leibniz' doctrine, of Locke's contention that identical and definitional truths, unlike the propositions of mathematics, are non-instructive and merely "trifling."

The third task will be a critical evaluation of Leibniz' theory of necessity, largely in terms of objections arising out of more recent philosophical inquiry. It will first be asked whether Leibniz' definition of necessary truth by reference to a formal principle can in any way provide for the connotations of inevitability or indispensability that have traditionally been regarded as essential to this notion. Secondly, I shall consider Leibniz' ability to account, on his theory, for the necessity of (a) negative necessary truths; (b) such apparently irreducible and indemonstrable propositions as "the red is not the green" or "every palpable body is visible" (the latter example having been suggested by Leibniz himself); and (c) the propositions of logic and mathematics (which recent reductionists have found insusceptible of proof without the assumption of non-identical primitives). This inquiry will reveal severe limitations in the support which Leibniz provided for his theory.

Finally, I shall examine the arguments which Leibniz offers in opposition to the conventionalistic views expounded by Hobbes and Locke (which views to some extent anticipate certain recent theories of necessary truth and a priori knowledge). It will be found that while Leibniz' objections to these "new philosophers," who would have truth "consist in words," are not without interest and brilliance, he seems ultimately to miss the significance of their observations concerning the nature of definition. Consequently, his attempted vindication of the "reality" and nonarbitrary character of necessary truths leaves many important questions unanswered.

I shall offer in conclusion some brief observations on the distinction between necessary and contingent truths as it appears in the total context of

Leibniz' philosophical system. It is my view that Leibniz' outright and irreconcilable inconsistencies on this questions have not been sufficiently noticed by commentators, with the inevitable results of much futile controversy.

NOTES

1. See for instance, Yvon Belaval, *Leibniz critique de Descartes* (Paris: Librarie Gallimard, 1960), p. 372. Belaval actually speaks of the definition of "possible," but, as will be seen below, the *necessary* (for Leibniz and his predecessors) is simply that of which the *opposite* is *not possible*.

CHAPTER 1

LEIBNIZ' DOCTRINE AND SOME HISTORICAL ANTECEDENTS

In this chapter I shall approach Leibniz' theory of necessity by first considering views elaborated by four of his predecessors--Aristotle, Aquinas, Nicholas of Autrecourt, and Hobbes. Each of these philosophers, as will become clear, anticipates Leibniz in respect of some of the elements of his doctrine. Except in the case of Hobbes, it will not be maintained that Leibniz was directly influenced, in arriving at his view of necessity, by study of the works of these writers. (Leibniz is known to have been a close student of Aristotle, and he was thoroughly educated in the scholastic tradition, but *direct* influence of particular philosophers on particular aspects of his doctrine of necessity cannot, in general, be established[1]). Nor, of course, is the examination of the positions of these four philosophers in any way intended to constitute a comprehensive survey of the development of philosophic treatments of the concept of necessity up to the time of Leibniz. The aim is rather the far more modest one of (1) indicating what elements of Leibniz' doctrine may assuredly be called "traditional," and from what "traditions" they respectively derive; and (2) illuminating certain important but subtle *differences* that obtain between Leibniz' doctrine and others similar to it, which have tended to pass unnoticed by commentators. (For example, it will be discovered that philosophers before Leibniz commonly held that necessity involves or consists in the "contradictoriness of the opposite," without arriving at Leibniz' view that necessary truths are those of which the denial can be reduced to a formal contradiction.)

I shall try to show that Leibniz' theory proceeds from a sort of marriage between the Aristotelian-Scholastic tradition on the one hand and the tradition of the geometers and Hobbes on the other hand. From the former come the notions, (1) that necessary truth differs from contingent truth in resting strictly on a *definitional* relation between the subject and predicate terms; (2) (a) necessity/impossibility can be defined by reference to *the principle of non-contradiction*, which (b) is at the same time, in some sense, the *first* principle of knowledge; and (3) that there is an important distinction between a truth's being necessary *absolutely* or in itself, and its being necessary only *hypothetically* or relative to certain premises. From the geometrical tradition derive, (1) emphasis on the importance of *demonstration* by means of *definitions and axioms* (with a clear indication of what is *assumed* in any proof); and (2) the view that the assumptions should be reduced to as *small* a number as possible--that it is valuable to attempt proofs even of apparently self-evident propositions.

1. ARISTOTLE

The conception of necessity.--Aristotle conceived of the problem of necessity as bound up with questions about the possibility and foundation of scientific knowledge. The latter questions, in turn, are approached from a metaphysical point of view. Aristotle asks not how we may come to know necessary truths, nor how we may recognize their necessity, but what connections in the *objects* of knowledge are necessary; what is therefore the appropriate subject matter for science. That which is not capable of being otherwise is necessarily as it is (τὸ μὴ ἐνδεχόμενον ἄλλως ἔχειν ἀναγκαῖόν φαμεν οὕτως ἔχειν)[2]. This is the primary sense of "necessary."[3] And only when we know that something is necessary in this sense do we say we have unqualified scientific knowledge of it (ἐπιστάσθαι οἰόμεθ' ἕκαστον ἁπλῶς).[4] "Consequently," Aristotle continues, "that of which there is unqualified scientific knowledge is something which cannot be otherwise" (ὥστε οὗ ἁπλῶς ἔστιν ἐπιστήμη, τοῦτ' ἀδύνατον ἄλλως ἔχειν).[5] Science, then, begins with necessary premises. But we must consider what these are.

Aristotle finds that necessary premises are those involving predication "καθ' αὐτό" or essential predication.⁶ Either what is predicated of the subject is part of the *ousia* of the subject (as line to triangle or point to line, for the *ousia* of the latter is in each case constituted by the former), or the subject is included in the explication of the nature (" τὸ τί ἐστιν ") of the predicate which is predicated of it. Thus to predicate straightness of a line is to predicate essentially, since straightness cannot be defined without reference to line (he gives several other examples).

It should be remarked that while Aristotle's account of essential predication and hence of necessity involves reference to definition, this by no means reflects a desire on his part to represent the problem of necessity as one having to do with a strictly linguistic connection between subject and predicate terms of a proposition, as opposed to the real connection between a "being" and its attributes. This is clear from the fact that his concept of definition is inseparably bound up with his concept of *ousia*, and from the fact that he conceives the problem as one concerning the objects of scientific knowledge. Leibniz will be found to differ from Aristotle to the extent of speaking almost exclusively of necessity as a property of propositions, the subject and predicate terms of which are related in a particular way. On the other hand, we shall also find that Leibniz would not go beyond Aristotle to the point of accepting a view of necessity which divorced it from the level of "being"; nor even, in the last analysis, of altogether relinquishing the notion of necessary connections *in rebus*.

The principle of non-contradiction.--In the discussion of necessity in the *Posterior Analytics* there is no reference to a formal criterion of necessity, such as Leibniz was to seek in the principle of identity or non-contradiction. In the *Metaphysics* Aristotle does describe the principle of non-contradiction as the first principle of all demonstration, "for this is naturally the starting point even for all the other axioms."⁷ Those who ask a proof even of this are simply uneducated:⁸ if this principle is denied there can be no reasons and *a fortiori* no proof of anything.⁹ But if we are to grasp the distance that separates Aristotle and Leibniz in their thoughts on this subject, it is necessary to observe the following points.

(1) As has been widely noticed, the principle of non-contradiction is not explicitly formulated by Aristotle as a formal or logical principle, but rather as a metaphysical principle.[10] He characterizes it, along with the other axioms, as a principle of being qua being (τοῦ ὄντος ἐστιν ᾗ ὄν).[11] Aristotle does not usually say that if a given proposition is true, then its negation is false, and no proposition can be both true and false.[12] Instead, he is accustomed to formulate the principle as follows: " τὸ γὰρ αὐτὸ ἅμα ὑπάρχειν τε καὶ μὴ ὑπάρχειν ἀδύνατον τῷ αὐτῷ καὶ κατὰ τὸ αὐτό" ("The same thing cannot belong to (subsist in, be attributed to) and be denied of the same thing in the same respect");[13] or, even more strikingly: " οὐκ ἐνδέχεται τὸ αὐτὸ καθ' ἕνα καὶ τὸν αὐτὸν χρόνον εἶναι καὶ μὴ εἶναι καὶ τἆλλα τὰ τούτου αὐτοῖς ἀντικείμενα τὸν τρόπον." ("It is not possible for the same thing at one and the same time to be and not be, and similarly for all other such opposites.")[14] Leibniz, on the other hand, almost always expresses the principle in a way that would be more acceptable to modern logicians. (It will be shown, however, that he does not wholly abandon the ontological formulation.)

(2) Aristotle does not mention the principle of identity as being on a par with or in any way involved with the principle of non-contradiction. This relative disregard of the principle of identity appears to have been the rule in the Aristotelian and Scholastic tradition down to the time of Leibniz.[15] (We shall see, however, that Nicholaus of Autrecourt, while not speaking of the principle of identity as such, emphasizes the point that propositions true by virtue of the principle of non-contradiction must be identities.)

(3) Most significantly, I think, Aristotle does not present the principle of contradiction as being in any way involved with the definition or criterion of necessity. He merely says that it is the most certain (βεβαιοτάτη) of all principles; the principle about which it is not possible to be mistaken (περὶ ἣν διαψευσθῆναι ἀδύνατον).[16] As already noted, Aristotle defines the necessary as "that which cannot be otherwise." Similarly, in *De Interpretatione* he equates "'necessary" with "opposite not possible" and "possible" with "opposite not necessary"[17] This is of course perfectly in accord with ordinary language, but does not go much beyond it. ("What does it mean for something to be necessary?" "Well, that it *has* to be that way.") There is an important

step--a step, I would say, from tautology to theory as well as from ordinary language to logic--between the assertion that something is necessary if it cannot be otherwise, and the two-fold contention that necessity applies to propositions, and that a proposition is necessarily true if and only if its negation implies a formal contradiction (or that its being necessary *means* that its negation implies a formal contradiction). This point may partially be rephrased as follows: "self-contradictory" is not itself a modal expression; hence, the effort to explain necessity in terms of self-contradiction is potentially illuminating in a way that an explanation using other modal terms ("cannot be otherwise") is not. (As we shall soon see, Leibniz was not the first to link necessity with self-contradiction. But I believe he was the first to attempt a systematic exploitation and development of this connection.)

It is true that Aristotle goes well beyond what would presumably be obvious to the ordinary speaker of Greek in his attempt to explain "cannot be otherwise" in terms of predication καθ' αὐτό But this explication in turn does not seem to point to any general or self-sufficient criterion. It rather appears to rely on the arrival at intuitive understanding through the citation of examples.

The contrast between absolute and hypothetical necessity.--Finally, we should note that there already appears in Aristotle's works a suggestion of the distinction between absolute and hypothetical necessity, which plays an important role in Leibniz' thought. In one brief passage, that is, Aristotle explicitly recognizes a distinction between what is necessarily true in itself, and what is necessary only in relation to certain premises.[18] In other passages, however, Aristotle explains the distinction in quite a different and logically less perspicuous way: he calls *things* that are necessitated by certain *ends* hypothetically necessary, and contrasts with these the (simple) necessity of things "that come about through the operation of nature."[19]

2. ST. THOMAS

St. Thomas' pronouncements on necessity, although of course strongly influenced by Aristotle, contain some interesting innovations which point to the direction in which the concept was to be developed by Leibniz.

Thomas' Aristotelian conception of necessity.--Much of the time Thomas seems to be at least as far away as was Aristotle from any general or formal characterization of necessity. Thus he echoes Aristotle in saying that the necessary is that which cannot not be (*"necesse est enim quod non potest non esse"*).[20] Something may be necessary, he says,

> in one way through an intrinsic principle [uno modo ex principio intrinseco]: either material, as when we say that everything composed of contraries is necessarily corrupted; or formal, as when we say that it is necessary to a triangle to have three angles equal to two right angles. And this is *natural and absolute necessity* [*necessitas naturalis et absoluta*].[21]

This necessity "ex principio intrinseco" seems to be approximately what he has in mind when he elsewhere speaks of something's being necessary *per se*.[22] From this he distinguishes necessity in virtue of an extrinsic principle (necessity *per aliud*.) This extrinsic principle may be either an end or an agent.[23] In the latter case we are dealing with a necessity of compulsion (*necessitas coactionis*). It is fairly evident, I think, that these distinctions do not answer many questions about the *nature* of necessity. (We may again notice reliance on the use of examples.) At the same time, such passages do not suggest an approach to necessity that is in any degree "proposition-oriented."

Necessity "ex habitudine terminorum."--Sometimes, however, Thomas expresses himself quite differently. Thus, in question 19, article 3 of the first part of the *Summa* he distinguishes two senses of necessity, "absolute" and "by supposition," and handles the distinction in a way reminiscent of Aristotle's remark in the *Prior Analytics*. He explains necessity "ex suppositione" by the assertion that while it is not necessary (absolutely) that Socrates sits, that he is sitting is a necessary consequence of the *supposition* "that he is sitting." What is more interesting, however, is the fact that he gives a straightforward and explicit account of absolute necessity as being judged of something "from the relation of the terms [ex habitudine terminorum]: in as much as the predicate is in the definition of the subject, as it is necessary for a man to be an animal; or because the subject is part of the account of the predicate [est de ratione praedicate], as it is necessary for a number to be even or odd." Of course this passage shows the influence of Aristotle's remarks in the *Posterior Analytics*, but it constitutes at least a slightly clearer statement that the necessary truth of a proposition consists in the subject and predicate terms being related by definition. There is, in particular, a notable absence of metaphysical overtones.

Necessity and opposition of terms.--In a similar vein, Thomas states that God is called omnipotent "because he can do anything that is possible absolutely" [potest omnia possibilia absolute], and adds:

> But something is said to be possible or impossible absolutely from the relation of the terms [ex habitudine terminorum]: it is possible when the predicate is not opposed to the subject [non repugnat subjecto], as [when it is said] that Socrates is sitting; it is absolutely impossible when the predicate is opposed to the subject, as [when it is said] that a man is an ass.[24]

The doctrine that there are, prior to creation, absolute impossibilities that are beyond the range of God's omnipotence was to be denied by Descartes[25] and vigorously reasserted by Leibniz. More to the point, however, is the fact that this passage follows the one previously quoted in explaining absolute impossibility in a general way, and by reference to the "relation of the terms," or the connection between subject and predicate. Thomas' use of the verb "repugnare" in this passage raises a question, when considered in conjunction with the assertion already quoted that the necessity of a truth is a result of the subject and predicate terms being related by *definition*. For Thomas, as for Aristotle, an impossible truth is one the denial of which is necessary.[26] But it is not clear that a proposition which is necessary simply in virtue of the "opposition of the terms" in its denial will always be a "definitional" truth. Thomas' own example ("a man is an ass") might be used to demonstrate this point, but a clearer instance is perhaps provided by the proposition, "red is blue." This might well be cited as a case of impossibility by virtue of opposition or incompatibility between the subject and predicate; therefore, its negation, "red is not blue," must be an instance of a necessary truth. That "not-blue" is in any way part of the definition of "red" is, however, extremely doubtful.[27] Thus Thomas, in so far as he leaves the term "repugnare" unexplained, fails to develop rigorously the implications of his own account of absolute necessity in terms of definition.

Necessity and self-contradiction.--This point must be borne in mind in evaluating the significance of the following very interesting passage from the same article:

> But nothing is opposed to [opponitur] the account [or "notion"] of being [rationi entis] except not-being. Therefore whatever in itself implies at the same time being and not-being is opposed to [repugnat] the account [or "notion"] of the absolutely possible, which is subject to the divine omnipotence. . . . Therefore whatever does not imply a contradiction is contained among those possibles in respect of which God is said to be omnipotent. But that which implies a contradiction is not contained under the divine omnipotence, because it cannot satisfy the account of possibility [quia non possunt habere possibilium rationem].[28]

Thomas here explicitly characterizes the impossible as that which implies a contradiction. Since, as has already been mentioned, he also holds that the denial of an impossible assertion is necessarily true, it would appear that his writings already contain the elements of Leibniz' basic definition of a necessary truth as one of which the opposite or negation is self-contradictory.

This suggestion requires, however, some very important qualifications. In the first place, as we have seen, it is by no means the case that Thomas always explains necessity in these terms. It is not easy to reconcile the definition of necessity in terms of contradiction with, for instance, the assertion that there is a kind of necessity that derives "ex principio intrinseco

... materiali."[29] Further, Thomas gives no indication that when he speaks of "implying a contradiction" he means "formally reducible to a proposition of the form, 'A is not-A' ". Indeed, a presumption that this is *not* what he has in mind is created by the proximity of the account of impossibility in terms of self-contradiction to the account in terms of "opposition" between subject and predicate, including the example, "a man is an ass." No further illumination on this point is to be derived from considering Thomas' remarks concerning the principle of non-contradiction itself. Although he follows Aristotle in regarding this principle as the first principle of demonstration, he does not give any indication of how it is to be used in demonstrating other truths, much less an actual example of a demonstration. In one place he says merely that this principle must be "understood" before any other principles can be understood;[30] elsewhere he writes that other principles are "reduced" to it, but does not elaborate on this remark.[31] Nor does he, in these passages, speak of the principle in connection with the problem of necessary truth.

We must therefore conclude that it is really not clear what connection Thomas sees between his contention that impossibility (or necessity) is ascribed *ex habitudine terminorum*, and the consequent reference, in one such passage, to definition; and his further proposal that the impossible is that which implies a contradiction. Nor does he explicitly relate his view of the primacy of the principle of non-contradiction to the doctrine that the impossible and the self-contradictory are the same. In particular, there seems to be no reason to suppose that Thomas had worked out the idea that the necessary truth of a proposition was to be established by reducing the negation of that proposition to a formal contradiction by means of a "chain of definitions." In these respects his doctrine is much less developed than that of Leibniz.

There is, however, another relevant respect in which Thomas' position differs from that of Leibniz: like Aristotle, he does not consider the principle of identity in discussing the principle of non-contradiction, and he also fails to draw the conclusion that if impossibility consists in self-contradictoriness, necessary truths will all be identities. That the latter notion had, however, entered the philosophical tradition well before the time of Leibniz, can be shown by an examination of some of the few extant writings of the fourteenth century Scholastic, Nicholas of Autrecourt.

3. NICHOLAS OF AUTRECOURT

Nicholas, in his *First and Second Letters to Bernard*, accepts the Aristotelian view that the principle of non-contradiction is the first principle of all demonstration, but criticizes Aristotle for not recognizing that this position entails an extremely limited view of the possibilities of human knowledge.[32] Nicholas argues (against Bernard of Arezzo) that if the only propositions we can know with certainty are those reducible to this principle, then we can never infer the existence of one thing from the existence of another thing.[33] From this conclusion he proceeds to a thorough "Humean" critique of the notions of cause and substance.[34] Fascinating as this critique is, we shall here only be concerned with his remarks concerning the principle of non-contradiction itself, and the immediate "corollaries" he draws from the premise that this principle is "what is found first at the origin of discourse."[35]

The primacy of the principle of non-contradiction.--Unlike Aristotle, Nicholas states the principle of non-contradiction exclusively in terms of truth (in one place) and of affirmation and negation (in another place) rather than in terms of "being":

> What is found first at the origin of discourse is this principle: Contradictories cannot at the same time be true.[36]

> A contradiction is the affirmation and negation of one and of the same etc., as is commonly said.[37]

Nicholas does not in any way *argue* for the point that this principle *is* the first (Bernard, at any rate, appears to have accepted this position):[38] he merely *asserts* that it is and that accordingly no other principle is prior to it, and it is prior to all others.[39] Nicholas appears to regard this assertion of the primacy of the principle as equivalent to the assertion that "all the certitude we have is resolved into this principle."[40] In any case, it is as the first principle of our *certitude* that he speaks of it almost throughout, rather than as a criterion of *necessity*. (In a letter to Egidius, however, he does characterize a necessary consequence as one which follows according to the principle of non-contradiction.[41])

Reducibility to the principle of non-contradiction.--Like Thomas, Nicholas speaks of the reducibility of all other certain truths to the principle of non-contradiction:

> From this it is clear that all our certitude is resolved into [resolvitur in] this principle, and it is not resolved into any other as a conclusion into a premise.[42]

And like Thomas, he does not give any account of the mechanics of such a reduction. That his point of view is somewhat closer to that of Leibniz than was Thomas', however, is suggested by the facts that, (1) he distinguishes between "mediate" and "immediate" reductions;[43] (2) he at one point likens the process of reduction to that carried out by a geometer;[44] (3) he speaks of the end result of reduction as a *formal* contradiction, i.e., as an affirmation and negation of a term of the term itself.[45] Nicholas also states that any syllogistic form is immediately reducible to the first principle,[46] although he does not offer such a demonstration (as Leibniz was to do).

The identity of propositions true by the principle.--Since Nicholas is not explicitly concerned with the definition of necessity, it can only be said with qualification that he maintains that all necessary truths are really identities. It is the case, however, that he repeatedly emphasizes the point that in all propositions true by virtue of the principle of non-contradiction--i.e., all certain propositions--the predicate will be either the same as the subject, or the same as a part of the subject:

> Fifth corollary [of axiom that the principle of non-contradiction is primary]: In every consequence [i.e., conditional] immediately reducible to the first principle the consequent and the whole antecedent, or the consequent and part of the antecedent, are really the same [idem realiter],

because if such were not the case, it would not be immediately evident that the antecedent and the opposite of the consequent cannot at the same time be true without contradiction.[47]

Similarly, he states as sixth corollary:

> In every evident conditional [omni consequentia] reducible to the first principle by as many intermediates as you like, the consequent is really the same as [idem realiter cum] the antecedent or with part of what is signified by the antecedent . . . .[48]

(This point is, of course, given such emphasis by Nicholas because it leads directly to the epistemological thesis he is seeking to establish: if "if A, then B" is a certain truth only when A and B can be shown to be the *same*, it follows that the existence of B can never be known from the existence of A, if B is different from A--i.e., the existence of one thing can never be inferred from the existence of another.)

Nicholas differs from Leibniz, however, not only in speaking of "certain" rather than of "necessary" truths, but also in the respect that he does not employ the *principle of identity* in his account of the foundations of certainty. He merely observes that a truth founded on the principle of non-contradiction will in fact be an identity--or rather that the predicate or consequence in such a truth will be "the same as" all or part of the subject or antecedent. Further, as has been indicated above, he does not show how such a demonstration is to be carried out, nor indicate that the means of reduction is to be the substitution of definiens for definiendum. Interest in rigorous formal demonstration of truths by means of primitive axioms and definitions does not, indeed, appear to have figured at all prominently in the Aristotelian-Scholastic tradition, in spite of the frequent remarks within this tradition concerning the "reducibility" of other true propositions to the principle of non-contradiction.

4. THOMAS HOBBES

Emphasis on the demonstration of truths by means of definition comes to the fore in the philosophic tradition with Thomas Hobbes, who was greatly stimulated in middle life by study of the work of Euclid.[49] Leibniz, moreover, is known to have read Hobbes' works with interest while still a young man.[50] The fact that Leibniz adapts a Hobbesian demonstration of one of Euclid's axioms and introduces it several times into his own writings is one indication of the real influence which the older philosopher had upon his thinking.[51] Leibniz was also both disturbed and stimulated by Hobbes' contention that truth rests on nothing more than human decisions about the use of words, and is therefore essentially "arbitrary." (Leibniz' reply to Hobbes on this point will be considered in chapter iv.)

Definition and demonstration.--For Hobbes, definitions, which have no other basis than the arbitrary decisions of human beings, are "primary principles":

> Now *primary* propositions are nothing but definitions, or parts of definitions, and these only are the principles of demonstration, being truths constituted arbitrarily by the inventors of speech, and therefore not to be demonstrated.[52]

Moreover,

> besides definitions, there is no other proposition that ought to be called primary, or (according to severe truth) be received into the number of principles. For those *axioms of Euclid*, seeing that they may be demonstrated, are no principles of demonstration. . . . [53]

A little further on Hobbes presents the following "definition of demonstration": "A demonstration is a syllogism, or series of syllogisms, derived and continued from the definitions of names, to the last conclusion."[54] As an example of the demonstration of an axiom, Hobbes offers the following proof of the Euclidean assumption that the *whole is greater than any part thereof*," to the end that the reader may know that these axioms are not indemonstrable, and therefore not principles of demonstration":

> *Greater* is defined to be that, whose part is equal to the whole of another. Now if we suppose any whole to be A, and a part of it to be B; seeing the whole B is equal to itself, and the same B is a part of A, therefore a part of A will be equal to the whole B. Wherefore, by the definition above, A is greater than B; which was to be proved.[55]

This proof is not set forth in the most perspicuous form; it might also be suggested that the initial definition of "greater" is so contrived as to be question-begging. What is of most interest here, however, is the fact that Hobbes, in sharp contrast to Aristotle and his Scholastic followers, is not content simply to *say* that axioms are derivable from (or reducible to) primitives: he undertakes to *illustrate* this point by producing an actual reduction. Even if one or two "reductions" are not enough to establish the thesis that all Euclidean axioms are susceptible of demonstration, Hobbes at least shows us what he has in mind when he speaks of the possibility of such demonstration. (Leibniz goes beyond Hobbes in presenting demonstrations of a number of logical and mathematical truths; although, as we shall find in chapter iii, he remains vulnerable to the charge of presenting far fewer than would be required to provide *substantial support* for his general reductionistic thesis.) Further, Hobbes makes clear, in both his general statements and this specific example, that *definition* is accorded the key role in his theory of demonstration. And this was perhaps the most important part of his doctrine for Leibniz. Although Leibniz takes issue with Hobbes' position that *only* definitions are required as primitives in demonstration, maintaining that the principle of identity or non-contradiction is also indispensable, he follows Hobbes both in according the substitution of definiens for definiendum an *essential* role in demonstration, and in accepting the geometrical ideal of restricting the class of primitives as much as possible. But the theory of demonstration is, for Leibniz, an inseparable part of his doctrine of necessity (necessary truths *are* those reducible by means of definitions to identity). We can therefore see the extent to which he drew, in arriving at this doctrine, on the geometrical tradition of Hobbes as well as on Aristotle and the Scholastics.

On the other hand, it would be a mistake to overemphasize the influence of Hobbes' ideas on Leibniz' doctrine of necessary truth. Partly to document this point, and partly to provide a basis for later discussion of Leibniz' opposition to Hobbesian conventionalism, we shall now consider two relevant points of obscurity in Hobbes' philosophy.

The nature of necessity.--For all Hobbes' emphasis on demonstration by definition, he does not explicitly connect such reductive demonstration with the concept of necessity. While he clears up with remarkable incisiveness the traditional muddle of necessary truth with necessity *in rebus*,[56] his own presentation of the concept of necessity is not altogether clear. He does make forcefully the point that necessity is a property of truths, and truth a property of propositions. To attribute necessity to a being is to become involved in what today is sometimes called a "category mistake," or as Hobbes would rather put it, an "incoherency of names."

> They err . . . that make this distinction between things that have being, that some of them *exist by themselves*, others by accident; namely, because *Socrates is a man* is a necessary proposition, and *Socrates is a musician* a contingent proposition, therefore they say some things exist necessarily or by themselves, others contingently or by accident; whereby, seeing *necessary, contingent, by* itself, *by accident*, are not names of things, but of propositions, they that say *any thing that has being, exists by accident*, copulate the name of a proposition with the name of a thing.[57]

But when Hobbes attempts to explain what the necessity of a necessarily true proposition consists in, he gives within one paragraph what appear to be three separate characterizations. (1) A proposition is necessarily true if there is nothing that "can at any time be conceived or feigned" to which the subject term is applicable and the predicate term is not: "as *man is a living creature* is a necessary proposition, because at what time soever we suppose the name *man* agrees with any thing, at that time *living-creature* also agrees with the same."[58] (2) A necessary proposition is one which can never be false. Thus "*every crow is black*; "which may perhaps be true now, but false hereafter," is a contingent truth. But in this formulation the modal term "can" (or "may") clearly indicates circularity.⁵⁹ Hobbes goes on to state that (3) "in every *necessary* proposition, the predicate is either equivalent to the subject, as in this, *man is a rational living creature*; or part of an equivalent name, as in this, *man is a living creature*. . . . " He adds that even if "every man is a liar" were "true always" the proposition would not be necessary, "because the word *liar* is no part of a compounded name equivalent to the name man."⁶⁰

Of these characterizations, (3) is the most interesting and probably the most basic, since it would presumably follow from the fact that P and Q are "equivalent" names, both that they "apply to the same things," and that "P is Q" is never false. Hobbes does not go out of his way to elucidate the notion of "equivalent names," however, and there are some questions that might be raised about it. For instance, Hobbes does not mention demonstration at all in this passage, nor does he mention definition. Does he wish to hold that the predicate term of a proposition is equivalent to the subject term (or is part of a term equivalent to the subject term) as long as the proposition is subject to demonstration by means of definitions? For example, does he think of "whole" and "greater than any of its parts" as equivalent terms? Is equivalence of one term to another something that may be (or may have to be) *demonstrated*, or is it, like ordinary synonymy, something that is ordinarily learned in the course of learning a language? We might also ask whether Hobbes thought a proposition could be necessarily true only when there exists a definition of the subject term. Many people, for example, would regard "Red is a color" as a necessary truth, and yet deny both that "color" is equivalent to "red" and that there is any expression equivalent to "red" of which the word "color" is a part. There is finally the question of how Hobbes would handle "negative necessary truths," such as "No vixen is male." Hobbes is mute on all these points; as Peters remarks, he does not seem to regard the distinction as important.⁶¹

The principles of non-contradiction and identity.--There are more serious obscurities to be found in Hobbes' conception of the status of the principles of non-contradiction and identity. On his own view they would apparently have to be either "definitions" (and hence "arbitrary") or demonstrable axioms; but it is hard to see how either account could be rendered cogent. It is worth noting that Hobbes employs without comment, in the demonstration quoted above of the axiom, "a whole is greater than any part thereof," the principle of identity in the form, "the whole of B is equal to itself." Elsewhere, while explicitly and forcefully denying that the principles of excluded middle and non-contradiction are principles of "being,"[62] he characterizes his own curious and highly misleading formulation of the two combined principles as the basis of all reasoning:

> The certainty of this axiom viz. *of two contradictory names, one is the name of anything whatsoever, the other not*, is the original and foundation of all ratiocination, that is, of all philosophy; and therefore it ought to be so exactly propounded, that it may be of itself clear and perspicuous to all men; as indeed it is, saving to such, as reading the long discourses made upon this subject by the writers of *metaphysics* . . . think they understand not when they do.[63]

(It is interesting that Hobbes combines the principle of excluded middle with that of non-contradiction: but note also that he does not introduce with these the principle of identity.) It would appear from this passage that Hobbes accepts the Aristotelian view that there can be no rational discourse unless the principle of non-contradiction is at least implicitly accepted. If so, besides the intrinsic implausibility of regarding the principle as a "definition," the further point would arise that the principle could not be properly regarded as "arbitrary" in the only sense that Hobbes gives this term--i.e., as a convention explicitly agreed upon among men, or dictated by some men to others.[64] For while we have at least some idea--some paradigm--of what it is to "agree upon a definition," or to "decree how a word is to be used," it is far from clear that any sense at all can be given to the expressions "agreeing to adopt the presuppositions of rational discourse," or "dictating the basic principle of ratiocination."

It will be important to bear in mind how vulnerable Hobbes' theory is at this point when we come to assess Leibniz' criticisms of his conventionalistic views. For one of Leibniz' principal objections is that Hobbes does not take account of the role played by the principle of non-contradiction (identity) in demonstration when he asserts that truth depends on "names."

In anticipation of Leibniz' criticisms it is further worthwhile to observe that Hobbes regards the principle of non-contradiction as governing the *creation* of "names." Thus, he writes in *Leviathan* that names "are but insignificant sounds" not only when unexplained by definition, but also,

> when men make a name of two Names, whose significations are contradictory and inconsistent; as this name, an *incorporeal body*, or (which is all one) an *incorporeal substance*, and a great number more. For whensoever any affirmation is false, the two names of which it is composed, put together and made one, signify nothing at all. For example, if it be a false affirmation to say *a quadrangle is round*, the word *round quadrangle* signifies nothing; but is a mere sound. So likewise if it be false, to say that vertue can be powered, or blown up and down; the words *In-powered vertue, In-blown vertue*, are as absurd and insignificant, as a *round quadrangle*.[65]

This passage, which I have not found to be cited by any of Leibniz' commentators, is important in several respects. In the first place, the latter part of the passage seems to suggest that Hobbes is advancing the view that all false propositions involve "inconsistent" predication[66]--a position closely related to the suggestion found in some of Leibniz' remarks (and regarded as his actual doctrine by many expositors) that all false propositions are virtually self-contradictory.[67] It is further interesting that, although Hobbes appears to make no distinction between the nonsense of an implicitly self-contradictory assertion and the nonsense of a proposition involving a "category mistake," he does explicitly recognize both forms of incoherent linking of "names." Leibniz, on the other hand, places great emphasis on the former and, in his mature work, ignores the latter altogether.[68] But what is most significant about this passage in its present context is simply the fact that Hobbes does explicitly state that two words cannot meaningfully be combined into one when their "significations" are mutually inconsistent. For, as we shall see, Leibniz' most frequently reiterated criticism of Hobbesian conventionalism (together with the one already mentioned above) turns on the point that our freedom arbitrarily to decide on the definition of a term is limited by the fact that a term may not be so defined that its definition contains a self-contradiction. But this point of Leibniz' is hardly different from what is here asserted by Hobbes himself: both maintain that a self-contradictory expression cannot be admitted into meaningful discourse.

5. SUMMARY OF THE FIRST FOUR SECTIONS

Although the four philosophers we have considered anticipate various elements of Leibniz' doctrine of necessary truth, none of them actually arrives at Leibniz' view that a necessary truth may be defined as a proposition of which the denial may be reduced to a formal contradiction by means of definitions. Aristotle, Thomas, and Nicholas all maintain the primacy of the principle of non-contradiction, and either assert or imply that it can serve as a basis for the demonstration of other truths (although it cannot be itself derived from any prior truth). Hobbes also seems to accept this view of the status of the principle of non-contradiction, although he does not show us a way to reconcile his position on this point with his statement that *definitions* are the only primitives to be employed in demonstration. None of these philosophers, however, explicitly proceeds from the contention that that principle of non-contradiction is the "first truth" to a definition of necessity in terms of reducibility to this principle. Thomas defined the impossible as the "self-contradictory," but he does not make clear that by "self-contradictory" he means in this context reducibility to a formal contradiction. Nicholas does speak explicitly of reduction to formal contradiction; but he is concerned throughout with the grounds of certainty, rather than the definition of necessity. And neither Thomas nor Nicholas stipulates that reduction of truths to the principle of non-contradiction is to be carried out in the geometrical mode by the formal procedure of substituting definiens for definiendum.

Hobbes, on the other hand, does advance a theory of demonstration of truths derived from the tradition of the geometers. He emphasizes the need to restrict the class of primitives: for Hobbes only definitions belong to this class. We have seen, moreover, that in his actual practice Hobbes anticipates Leibniz' doctrine of demonstration more fully than in his professed theory, in as much as he does implicitly employ the principle of identity as well as definitions in providing an example of the formal demonstration of a Euclidean axiom. Unlike Leibniz, however, Hobbes does not in any way incorporate his theory of demonstration into his account of necessary truth.

We have also noticed that these philosophers differ from Leibniz in not treating the principle of identity together with the principle of non-contradiction, although Nicholas points out that the denial of a proposition will be formally self-contradictory only if the predicate of the original proposition is in fact identical with all or part of the subject.

Finally we have observed, in studying these four philosophers, some signs of an increasing tendency to treat necessity as a property of truths, based on the formal relation of predicate to subject term, rather than as a relationship obtaining *in rebus*; and also to express the principle of non-contradiction as governing the relationship between affirmative and negative propositions or positive and negative terms, rather than between "being" and "non-being."

6. LEIBNIZ' DEFINITION OF NECESSITY

Absolute vs. hypothetical and moral necessity.--Leibniz incorporates within his system the traditional distinction between absolute and hypothetical necessity. Leibniz tends to treat the two types of necessity as mutually exclusive: truths are hypothetically necessary if they are merely the necessary consequences of truths or assumptions not themselves absolutely necessary. This distinction plays an important role in his metaphysico-theological writings,[69] in which he argues that laws specifically obtaining in this world are *merely* hypothetically necessary: they follow mediately (through more general laws) or immediately from a few very general truths concerning God's initial decisions about what sort of world to create.[70] Truths describing God's initial decisions, however, are not themselves absolutely necessary: it is not absolutely impossible that God should have made different decisions than he did.[71] Leibniz also introduces the concept of *moral* necessity in these writings. This necessity characterizes decisions: it is morally necessary that "a wise being [choose] the best, and every mind [follow] the strongest inclination."[72] It is thus *morally* necessary that God made the decisions that he did, since they were in fact the best decisions he could make. Moral necessity, too, is consistently opposed to absolute necessity.

In this essay, however, I shall be concerned only with clarifying the concept of *absolute* necessity. It is always absolute necessity which he has in mind when he offers a definition of the term "necessary" itself. The concept of absolute necessity can, moreover, be regarded as the most basic on the grounds that, while it can be defined and explained without reference to hypothetical or moral necessity, it is not clear that the latter concepts can be explained without reference to it. (This is obvious in the case of the hypothetically necessary, which is simply a consequence that follows with absolute necessity from a premise (or premises) not absolutely necessary itself (themselves). But it is also notable that in attempting to explain moral necessity Leibniz usually falls back on formulae which involve negative references to absolute necessity: e.g., he characterizes it as involving "certainty and infallibility, but not an absolute necessity."[73])

The definition of (absolute) necessity.--Leibniz begins with the traditional equation of "necessary" with "opposite impossible," and of "impossible" with "self-contradictory":

> A necessary proposition is one of which the opposite is not possible, or the opposite of which having been assumed, a contradiction is arrived at by resolution.[74]

The first step seems to raise no problems and to call for no justification. But the definition of "impossible" in terms of self-contradictoriness becomes, in Leibniz' philosophy, both interesting and problematic.

That "self-contradictory" constitutes for Leibniz simply the definitional equivalent of "impossible" is evident from his repeated linking of the two words with terms like "seu," "sive," and "c'est à dire,"[75] as well as from numerous passages in Couturat's edition of fragments (for instance) which clearly have the role of setting forth definitions in the context of systematic expositions of logical calculi, and are of the form: "impossible assertions are those which can be reduced to contradiction, [etc.]."[76] We have, moreover, Leibniz's express statement to this effect in the *Théodicée*, where he quotes Bayle's remark that the Spinozists:

> are made uncomfortable by having it known that they overthrow a maxim as universal and as evident as this: Whatever implies a contradiction is impossible, and whatever does not imply a contradiction is possible.[77]

After a word of praise for Bayle, Leibniz continues:

> I shall add only that what has just been characterized as a maxim is actually the definition [est même la définition] of the possible and the impossible.[78]

The assertion that "self-contradictory" is nothing but the definition of "impossible" becomes more or less interesting, depending on whether "self-contradictory" is understood in a relatively vague and "popular" or a relatively strict and technical sense. Thus, in St. Thomas' equation of "impossible" with "self-contradictory," the latter term does not seem to be accorded any very precise signification. It is not clear that "a self-contradictory assertion" connotes either more or less to Thomas than "an assertion involving incompatible predication." The latter expression is, in turn, left on a more or less intuitive level, as I have already remarked in connection with Thomas' use of the verb "repugnare."[79] If we go no further than this, the definition of "impossibility" in terms of self-contradiction does not seem to be either very controversial or very interesting.

Contradictoriness and formal demonstration.--In Leibniz' work, however, "self-contradictory" is not allowed to stand as a mere synonym for the imprecise term "incompatible." It is rather given precise formal signification. The principle of non-contradiction may according to Leibniz be expressed in the partially symbolic form, "A is not not-A."[80] A self-contradictory proposition is accordingly one entailing a denial of this principle: i.e. a proposition which is either expressly of the form "A is not-A," or can be transformed to a proposition of this form by a series of substitutions of definientia for definienda.[81] (Propositions of the form "AB is not-A", in which the predicate is the negation of *part* of the subject, while sometimes distinguished by Leibniz from geometrical truths in which the predicate is the negation of the whole subject, are also counted by him as formal self-contradictions.[82]) Leibniz thus combines in his notion of self-contradiction a formal conception of express self-contradiction ("A is not-A") with a formal geometrical understanding of reduction to express self-contradiction (reduction by substitution of definition.)

But once "self-contradictory" is understood in this formal sense, its acceptability as a *definition* of "impossible" is by no means unchallengeable. The very novelty and interest of Leibniz' account of necessity indicates that this is at least not what either non-philosophers or philosophers had commonly regarded as the *meaning* of "impossible" when they used the word. A suggestion that Leibniz' account of necessity is "true by definition" in an uncontroversial sense must rely on an equivocation between two senses of "self-contradictory": a traditionally vague sense in which the term really is roughly equivalent to "impossible" even in ordinary speech, and a more technical, strictly formal sense, whose equivalence to "impossible" must be regarded as a sort of theoretical proposition, rather than as an established fact of ordinary usage.

What might lead, then, to the citing of "self-contradictory" in the stricter sense as the definition of "impossible"? Perhaps the most sympathetic way of looking at this matter is the following. We note that "self-contradictoriness" (in *some* sense) has traditionally been taken as the defining property of the impossible, and we ask what this traditional view can amount to. What does it add to our understanding of the impossible to say that impossibility is constituted by self-contradictoriness? Little, surely, if "self-contradictory assertion" is taken as a mere *synonym* of "impossible assertion."

For the definition to be philosophically helpful, we must be able to specify in other terms what we mean by "self-contradictory." This need suggests that a formal interpretation of the expression would be desirable. If we understand "self-contradictory" as equivalent to "expressly or implicitly[83] of the form 'A is not-A,'"[84] we arrive at a clear and specific account of what an impossible assertion *is*, which does not invite charges of circularity by employing a modal term in the definiens. And that such an interpretation would "work" is suggested by the fact that the principle of contradiction had since Aristotle been regarded as *the first principle* of logic--as logically prior "even to all the other axioms." On the mathematician's understanding of the nature and role of an axiom, and of the meaning of "logical priority" (which Leibniz clearly shares),[85] the doctrine that the principle of non-contradiction is *the first principle* of logic implies that other logically true propositions can be *derived from it by means of definitions*.[86] But that the traditional necessary truths, including, of course, mathematical propositions, are in fact susceptible of demonstration by the reduction of their negations to contradiction is not an obvious fact, but something that must be *shown*. It is in this respect that Leibniz' doctrine of necessary truth constitutes an interesting and significant philosophical theory. (The extent to which he *is* able to validate his theory by providing such reductions will be considered in chapter iii.)

Leibniz' doctrine in fact involves a merging of the concept of necessity derived from tradition with the geometrical ideal of rigorous proof. To reduce the negation of a proposition to a formal self-contradiction is the only way to establish the necessity of that proposition; it is also, on Leibniz' view, the most rigorous way of establishing its truth. For questions concerning the certainty of traditional necessary truths are reduced to the comparatively manageable question of the certainty of the principle of non-contradiction (and this principle, as we shall see, Leibniz takes to be certain in the highest possible degree). The aim and method of the undertaking of reduction involves, moreover, eradication or at least relaxation of the traditional boundaries between logic and mathematics--a consequence which Leibniz openly embraces.[87]

Necessity and the principle of identity.--A final important aspect of Leibniz' definition of necessity must now be considered. We have seen that Nicholas of Autrecourt observed that propositions of which the negations are self-contradictory will themselves be identities. Leibniz goes beyond this, however: he treats the principle of identity ("A is A") as simply the affirmatively expressed form of the principle of non-contradiction ("not (A is not-A)"),[88] and is hence able to treat all formal identities as primitive truths.[89] This leads to a more direct way of defining necessity. A necessary truth is one of which the *opposite* or negation is or may be reduced to an express *contradiction*; but once the principle of identity is accepted on a par with the principle of non-contradiction, a necessary truth may with equal completeness (but greater simplicity) be defined as a proposition which *itself* is or may be reduced to an express *identity*.

> Necessary truths are those which can be reduced to identities, or the opposites of which can be reduced to contradictions.[90]

I think it is significant, however, that Leibniz seldom defines necessity by reference to identity alone. He usually explicitly cites reducibility to identity *as the equivalent of* the reducibility of the opposite to contradiction. And in fact it is much more often the latter (contradiction) rather than the former (identity) that he mentions first or otherwise emphasizes. This evident tendency to explain the identity criterion in terms of the criterion of contradiction is striking enough to suggest that Leibniz implicitly accepts the existence of a stronger definitional link between impossibility and contradiction than between necessity and identity. The equation of "necessary" with "identical" does not, indeed, share the apparent obviousness of the equation of "impossible" with "self-contradictory." The explanation of this difference may well be that "identity" (in the sense of identical truth or assertion) is almost exclusively a technical term with a precise formal signification, whereas "self-contradiction" (as I have pointed out above) is not. But since Leibniz is in fact *using* "self-contradictory" in as strict a sense as "identical," the apparent difference is in the case of his doctrine illusory (which is also to say that *neither* aspect of the identity-contradiction criterion is "obvious.") Here there is, perhaps, a slight suggestion that Leibniz himself unconsciously relies on the broader, traditional understanding of "self-contradictory" in "putting over" his doctrine of necessary truth, even though the content and interest of his theory derive from the fact that he is ostensibly using "self-contradictory" in a narrower, technical sense.

7. CONCLUSION

We have seen that Leibniz, incorporating elements from both the Scholastic tradition and the tradition of the geometers, maintains the position that all necessary truths are derivable by the formal substitution of definition from the principle of identity. He remarks, in particular, that "this single principle is sufficient to demonstrate every part of arithmetic and geometry, that is, all mathematical principles."[91] He also writes that "Logic is as susceptible of demonstration as geometry."[92] The question of what other general classes of truths Leibniz regards as derivable from identities by means of definitions cannot, I believe, be answered with complete precision and certainty. In an early letter he indicates that "a large number" of the propositions of metaphysics, physics, and ethics are of this type.[93] It is certain, however, that by the end of his life he had come to regard all physical laws as contingent,[94] and I find some unclarity in his later writings about the status of metaphysics and morality.[95] For the purpose of the ensuing discussion, in any case, it is not essential to go beyond the fact that Leibniz explicitly and consistently characterizes the truths of mathematics and logic as derivable from identity.[96]

Having thus established the general outlines of Leibniz' doctrine of necessary truth, we must now proceed to a clarification and evaluation of the theory from various points of view. In the next chapter, therefore, we shall consider Leibniz' vindication of his doctrine against the chief opposition of his own century: the intuitionism of Descartes and Locke. These philosophers polemicized against both the geometrical ideal of formal demonstration of all axioms, and the scholastic insistence on the primacy of the principle of non-contradiction. They were led by their experience of the sterility of scholastic logic to elevate intuition of self-evidence above formal proof. Against them

Leibniz, while conceding the limitations of Scholasticism,[97] argues for the interest and value of revealing the "source" of necessary truths in the principle of non-contradiction (identity), and decries the unscientific subjectivism consecrated by the Cartesian methodology. The aim of our discussion will not be to arrive at a clear decision between the two opposed points of view, but rather to clarify the basis and nature of the controversy, and to reveal some fundamental conceptual differences which underlie it. (This clarification will, however, lead to the negative conclusion that Locke's detailed anti-reductionistic arguments cannot be regarded as effectively discrediting Leibniz' position.)

A more systematic critical evaluation of Leibniz' doctrine will then be undertaken in the third chapter.

NOTES

1. Detailed accounts of Leibniz' early studies may be found, for instance, in Kuno Fischer, *Geschichte der neuern Philosophie*, II (Heidelberg: Carl Winter's Universitäts-Buchhandlung, 1889) pp. 29-43, and Yvon Belaval, *Leibnitz: initiation à sa philosophie* (Paris: Librairie Philosophique J. Vrin, 1962), chaps. ii-iii. Cf. letter to Remond, 1714 (G.III.606): Etant enfant j'appris Aristote, at même les Scholastiques ne me rebutérent point. . . . "
2. *Metaphysics* v. 5. 1015^a 34. Translations throughout the paper are mine unless otherwise indicated.
3. *Ibid.*, 35-36.
4. *Posterior Analytics* i. 2. 71^b 9.
5. *An. Post.* i. 2. 71^b 15-16; cf. 4. 73^a 21.
6. *Ibid.*, 4, esp. 73^a 34-73^b 3, and 73^b 3, and 73^b 16-14. This interpretation of Aristotle's position on the nature of necessary premises is advanced by Mrs. Kneale (see William and Martha Kneale, *The Development of Logic* [Oxford: Clarendon Press, 1962], pp. 94-95), and seems to me to be clearly supported by the text of the *Posterior Analytics*. It should be mentioned, however, that some commentators maintain that Aristotle regarded all predicates which *always* belong to a subject as necessarily connected with that subject, even when the relation between subject and predicate is not "essential." (See, for instance, G.E.M. Anscombe and P.T. Geach, *Three Philosophers* [Ithaca: Cornell University Press, 1961], pp. 34-35.)
7. *Met.* iv. 3. 1005^b 33-34 (Oxford Translation).
8. *Ibid.* 1006^a 5-8.
9. Thus Aristotle says that the principle can be proved "negatively" (elsewhere [*Met.* ix. 5. 1062^a 3] "ad hominem" or "relative to the person present"), "if our opponent will only say something. . . . The starting-point for all such arguments is not the demand that our opponent shall say that something either is or is not (for this one might perhaps take to be a begging of the question), but that he shall say

something which is *significant* both for himself and for another; for this is necessary, if he really is to say anything. For, if he means nothing, such a man will not be capable of reasoning, either with himself or with another. But if any one grants this, demonstration will be possible; for we shall already have something definite. The person responsible for the proof, however, is not he who demonstrates but he who listens; for while disowning reason he listens to reason" (*Ibid.* 11-26 [Oxford translation]). These remarks of Aristotle's, like others on the same subject (cf. *Met.* ix. 5) are more than slightly obscure, but the main point appears to be that reasoning is simply meaningful discourse; and that there can be no meaning or significance in our words and sentences, unless the affirmation is admitted to exclude the denial. Similarly, at *Met.* iv. 4. Aristotle observes that the argument with the person who denies the principle of non-contradiction is an argument "about nothing," for he "says nothing," in that he says not that "it is so" nor that "it is not so," but that it is both; and then again that it is neither. As will be seen, the remark that to deny the principle of non-contradiction is to "say nothing" is again made by Leibniz.

10. Cf. Ross's commentary on *Met.* 1005^b 19 (*Aristotle's Metaphysics*, ed. W.D. Ross [Oxford: Clarendon Press, 1958], I, p. 264); also Anscombe and Geach, *op. cit.*, p. 39.
11. *Met.* iv. 3. 1005^a 24.
12. There are exceptions, however. See, e.g., *Met.* iv. 6. 1001^b 20f.
13. *Met.* iv. 3. 1005^b 19-20.
14. *Met.* xi. 5. 1061^b 36-1062^a 2.
15. Cf. Otto Saame, *Der Satz vom Grund bui Leibniz* (Mainz: Hanns Krach, 1961), p. 16: "Dass die Zusammenfassung von Identität und Kontradiktion zu *einem* Prinzip in der damaligen Zeit neu war, kann ein Blick auf die "Schulmetaphysiker" des 17. Jahrhunderts zeigen, die haupstächlich das Prinzip der Kontradiktion herausstellen." He gives several references, which I have generally been able to confirm, and adds: "Der Begriff der Identität ist natürlich in der Philosophie schon lange bekannt, auch wurde er schon zum Prinzip erhoben, aber

in engen Zusammenhang gebracht mit dem Prinzip des Widerspruchs wurde er erstmals durch Leibniz."

16. *Met.* iv. 3. 1005^b 11-12.
17. *De Int.*, chaps. 12 and 13.
18. *Prior Analytics* i. 10. 30^b 30-40. Cf. Kneales, *op. cit.*, pp. 93-94.
19. *Physics* ii. 9. 199^b 34-200^b 11 (Oxford translation); see also *De Partibus Animalium* i. 1. 639^b 20-640^a 10. Cf. W.D. Ross, Aristotle (New York: Meridian Books, 1959), p. 81. Both of these passages are complicated and rather obscure.
20. *Summa theologica*, I, q. 82, a. 1 c.
21. *Ibid.*
22. *Ibid.*, q. 41, a. 2 ad 5, for instance.
23. *Ibid.*, q. 82 a. 1 c; cf. III, q. 46, a. 1 c.
24. *Ibid.*, q. 25, a. 3 c. Cf. *Ibid.*, q. 46, a. 1.
25. Also by certain Scholastics. Cf. Gottfried Martin, *Leibniz: Logic and Metaphysics*, trans. K.J. Northcott and P.G. Lucas (Manchester: Manchester University Press, 1964), p. 6.
26. See his *Commentary on the Metaphysics of Aristotle*, trans. John P. Rowan ("Library of Living Catholic Thought," Chicago: Henry Regnery Company, 1961), v. L.14: C954-976 (p. 372).
27. This sort of proposition will be further discussed in chapter iii, in connection with the Leibnizian theory of necessity.
28. *Summa theologica, loc. cit.*
29. See above, p. 15.
30. *Commentary on the Metaphysics of Aristotle*, iv. L. L.6: C 596-610 (p. 243). Later in the same work (xi. L.5: C 2211-2224 [vol. II, p. 794] Thomas adds the assertion that this is the first principle "because its terms, *being* and *non-being*, are the first to be apprehended by the intellect." The suggestion of *psychological* priority implicit in this account appears to be Thomistic rather than Aristotelian. Similarly, where Aristotle says only that the principle of non-contradiction is not demonstrable, Thomas adds that it *comes naturally* to the knower; that it is not *acquired* through a process of reasoning (*ibid.*, p. 243). These scholastic improvements on Aristotle will be seen reflected in various

ways in the writings of Descartes, Locke, and Leibniz to be considered below.

31. *Summa theologica*, IIae, IIa, g. 1, a. 7.
32. *Epistola magistri Nicolai de Autricort ad Bernardum* [Second Letter to Bernard] in Joseph Lappe: *Nicolaus von Autrecourt: sein Leben, seine Philosophie, seine Schriften* ("Beitraege zur Geschichte der Philosophie des Mittelalters, Bd. VI, Heft 2, Münster: Aschendorffschen Buchhandlung, 1908), pp. 12*-13* (Lappe paginates the texts of Nicholas with numerals to which asterisks are added, in distinction from the ordinary pagination of his own discussion.) The first two letters to Bernard are published in a translation by E.A. Moody in *Medieval Philosophy*, ed. Herman Shapiro (New York: Modern Library, 1964), pp. 510-526. Although I have occasionally drawn upon Moody's translations, the ones provided here are substantially my own.
33. *Ibid.*, p. 9*.
34. First two letters to Bernard, *passim* (Lappe, pp. 2*-14*); also *Epistola Nicholay ad Egidium* (Lappe, pp. 24*-30*). Cf. Julius R. Weinberg, *Nicholaus of Autrecourt* (Princeton: Princeton University Press, 1948), chaps. ii-v.
35. Second Letter to Bernard (Lappe, p. 2*).
36. *Ibid.*
37. *Ibid.*, p. 7.
38. *Ibid.*
39. *Ibid.*
40. *Ibid.*
41. *Epistola ad Egidium* (Lappe, p. 26*.)
42. Second Letter to Bernard, *ibid.*
43. *Ibid.*, p. 8*.
44. *Ibid.*
45. *Ibid.*, pp. 9*-10*.
46. *Ibid.*, p. 8*.
47. *Ibid.* (See Moody's note on consequentia, *Medieval Philosophy*, p. 519.)
48. *Ibid.*, p. 9*.
49. Cf. Richard Peters, *Hobbes* (Penguin Books: 1956), p. 21.

50. See Couturat's appendix on Leibniz and Hobbes, *Log.*, pp. 456-472. Also, Kurt Huber, *Leibniz* (München: R. Oldenbourg, 1951), p. 24. Huber indicates that Leibniz was directed to the study of Hobbes by Eberhard Weigel, an eminent philosopher and mathematician, who was his teacher at the University of Jena in 1663. Weigel, a "Renaissance Pythagorean," was himself extremely interested in Euclidean method (*ibid.*, p. 23.)

51. Cf. *Log.*, p. 204. Laudatory references to Hobbes are found in an early work of Leibniz': the *Ars Combinatoria* (see, e.g., G. IV, p. 64).

52. *Concerning Body*, Part I, iii, 9. This English translation of *De corpore*, which was made during Hobbes' lifetime, may be found in *The English Works of Thomas Hobbes*, ed. W. Moleworth, vol. I (London: John Bohn, 1839).

53. *Ibid.*, vi, § 13.

54. *Ibid.*, § 16.

55. *Ibid.*, viii, § 25. As Leibniz remarks more than once, attempts to demonstrate Euclidean axioms and postulates are also to be found in the works of geometers. He is fond of contrasting the rigorous proofs sought after by this tradition with the "self-evidence" criterion favored by the scholastics and consecrated by Descartes and his followers, to the disadvantage of the latter thinkers. For instance, he writes: "Vous trouverez en cent lieux que les Philosophes de l'Ecole ont dit que ces propositions [the axioms] sont evidentes *ex terminis* aussitôt qu'on entend les termes. ... Mais les Géometres ont bien fait d'avantage: c'est qu'ils ont entrepris de les demontrer bien souvent." He mentions Thales, Apollonius, and Proclus as having reportedly attempted such demonstrations, as well as a contemporary, M. Roberval. (*N. E.*, IV, xii, § 14; cf. *Animadversiones in partem generalem principiorum Cartesianorum*, S., pp. 17-18.

56. See, besides passages already quoted, Aristotle, *Prior Analytics* i. 15. 34^a 13-16.

57. *Concerning Body*, I, v, § 9. Hobbes is equally forceful in distinguishing definition from essence ("definition is not the essence of any thing, but a speech signifying what we conceive of the essence thereof"

[*Ibid.*, § 7]), and implication from cause (*Ibid.*, iii, § 20). Whether he is altogether consistent in observing his own distinctions is another question. Thus in *The Questions Concerning Liberty, Necessity, and Chance* he writes: "I put necessity for an impossibility of not being." (English Works, ed. Molesworth, vol. V (1841, p. 48.)

58. *Concerning Body*, I, iii, § 10.
59. This objection may perhaps also be brought against (1), unless the "can" is there taken exclusively as referring to psychological ability for which there are definite tests.
60. *Concerning Body, loc. cit.*
61. Peters, *op. cit.*, p. 56: "Hobbes . . . does not develop this distinction and does not think it important in his account of scientific knowledge; for science is concerned only with what he calls necessary truths." This seems a rather strange "explanation"!
62. *Concerning Body*, I, ii, § 8: "They that say *the same thing cannot both be, and not be*, speak obscurely; but they that say, *whatsoever is, either is, or is not*, speak also absurdly and ridiculously."
63. *Ibid.*
64. Cf. *Concerning Body*, I, ii, 4; also I, iii, 8. In the former passage Hobbes concedes that some names were imposed arbitrarily by *God*, but this does not seem materially to affect the point at issue.
65. *Leviathan*, Part I, iv (Oxford reprint of the edition of 1651 [Oxford: Clarendon Press, 1958], pp. 30-31.)
66. This is not, however, a proposition that Hobbes consistently holds. For instance, he writes in *Concerning Body*, I, iii, § 7: "A *true* proposition is that, whose predicate contains, or comprehends its subject, or whose predicate is the name of every thing, of which the subject is the name; as *man is a living creature* is therefore a true proposition, because whatsoever is called *man*, the same is also called *living creature*; and *some man is sick*, is true, because *sick* is the name of *some man*. That which is not true, or that whose predicate does not contain its subject, is called a *false* proposition, as *man is a stone*." If we overlook the idiosyncracies of Hobbes' terminology, and the fact that in the *example* he gives of a false proposition, the two names put together in

fact do "signify nothing at all," this characterization at least *appears* to leave room for propositions whose truth or falsity does not in any way follow from the meaning of the subject and predicate terms.

67. Whether or not this may be said to be Leibniz' actual position will be considered in the conclusion of this essay.

68. Leibniz does take note in the *Ars Combinatoria* of some of Hobbes' general restrictions on the linking of "names" which are independent of the exclusion of the formally self-contradictory (G., IV, p. 46).

69. Especially the *Discours de Métaphysique*, the Arnuald correspondence, and the *Théodicée*.

70. See *T.*, p. 52; *O. F.*, pp. 18-20.

71. See, e.g., *Discourse de Métaphysique*, xiii (G. IV, p. 438); *N. E.* II, xxi, § 8.

72. Fifth letter to Clarke, § 4 (in *The Leibniz-Clarke Correspondence*, ed. H. G. Alexander ["Philosophical Classics"; Manchester: Manchester University Press, 1956], p. 56). Clarke's translation. Cf. *Discours de Métaphysique, loc. cit., T.*, p. 38.

73. Fifth letter to Clarke, § 9 (*loc. cit.*, p. 57). Cf. *Discours de Métaphysique, loc. cit.* Leibniz also states repeatedly that the reason or motive which determines any given choice "inclines without necessitating"--i.e., without rendering it absolutely necessary that the choice be made in that particular way (see e.g., *T.*, 419). As the Arnauld correspondence testifies, the notion that God's choice could be determined in advance with "certainty and infallibility" and yet not be absolutely necessary was found extremely obscure by Leibniz' contemporaries. More recently, A. O. Lovejoy has argued that the concept of moral necessity is nonsensical (*The Great Chain of Being* [Cambridge: Harvard University Press, 1957], pp. 172-173).

74. *O. F.*, p. 374.

75. *Ibid.*, p. 374, *T.*, p. 228, etc.

76. *O. F.*, p. 387 and *passim*.

77. *T., loc. cit.*

78. *Ibid.* After about 1671 Leibniz consistently insists upon a distinction between definitions on the one hand and truths or axioms on the other hand. Cf. *N. E.*, IV, vii, § 6. At the very beginning of his career, however, he had accepted the Hobbesian characterizations of first principles as definitions (Cf. *Log.*, pp. 184 ff).

79. See also Descartes' reply to Objections II: "All impossibility or . . . implication of contradiction [implicantia] consists only in our concept or thought, which cannot join together ideas that are mutually opposed [mutuo adversantes]. . . . " (*Oeuvres de Descartes*, ed. Charles Adam and Paul Tannery [Paris: Leopold Cerf, 1897-1910], vol. VII, p. 152.) Hobbes also seems not explicitly to distinguish technically self-contradictory expressions from other forms of "absurd and insignificant" predication, but to rank all together under "contradictory and inconsistent names." (See above, p. 37.) A contemporary parallel may perhaps be found in A. J. Ayer's use of "self-contradictory" in *Language, Truth, and Logic* (2d ed. revised; New York: Dover, n.d.). Ayer maintains that the propositions of logic and mathematics are necessary in that we cannot abandon them "without contradicting ourselves, without sinning against the rules which govern the use of language, and so making our utterances self-stultifying" (p. 77; see also p. 80 and p. 84). On p. 95 he asserts that "the one thing we may not do" is maintain a set of hypotheses which are "incompatible" or mutually self-contradictory. At the same time he vigorously denies (p. 81) that any analytic proposition including the law of non-contradiction is prior to others, or the ground of their validity. It must therefore be concluded that when Ayer says necessary truths are necessary because their denial involves us in contradiction, he is understanding "contradiction" in a broad, non-technical sense: otherwise he would have to be saying that necessary truths are necessary because they are derivable from the principle of non-contradiction (and therefore contradicting himself!).

80. See second letter to Clarke, § 1, p. 15; also Martin *op. cit.*, p. 4. Alternatively, Leibniz formulates the principle as follows: "The principle of contradiction is in general: a proposition is either true or

false; which includes two statements; one, that the true and the false are not compatible in the same proposition, or that a proposition cannot be true and false at the same time. The other, that the opposite or the negation of the true and the false are not compatibles, or that there is no middle term between the true and the false . . . ." (*N. E.*, IV, 2, § 1. Note that the principle of excluded middle is included in this formulation.) Sometimes, however, Leibniz states the principle in terms of *being* and *not-being*: cf. e.g., *O. F.*, p. 515.

81. *O. F.*, p. 259, 371, etc. As will be noted below, this formulation requires slight modification to take care of negative propositions.
82. Cf. e.g., *N. E.*, *loc. cit.*
83. "Implicitly of the form 'A is not-A' " meaning, again, reducible to this form by substitution of definition.
84. Or "p and not-p," where "p" stands for a proposition: see note 73.
85. Cf. *Monadologie*, §§ 33-34 (*G.*, VI, p. 612).
86. It is not, of course, claimed that Leibniz actually reasoned in this way in arriving at his doctrine. The aim is simply to illuminate the significance of the doctrine by indicating its ties with, and advances from, traditional views.
87. Leibniz' aim is the "reduction of mathematics to logic," but his conception of logic is a thoroughly mathematical one, involving emphasis on the development of convenient symbolism, attention to the introduction of definitions, and a notion of logical demonstration which regards reduction to axioms through the substitution of equivalents as more basic than syllogistic reasoning. Couturat has provided a thorough and lucid exposition of these points (*Log.*, chaps. iv, vi, and vii). He writes, for instance: "[Leibniz] a découvert que la méthode mathématique peut s'appliquer aussi aux objets de l'entendement pur, c'est-à-dire aux notions abstraites et métaphysiques: c'est là la véritable Logique . . . ." (P. 239) Also (p. 317): "Leibniz a eu le mérite d'apercevoir . . . qu'il y a une Mathématique universelle dont toutes les sciences mathématiques relèvent pour leurs principes et leurs théorèmes les plus généraux, et que cette Mathématiques rentre à ce titre tout entière dans la Logique

formelle. Mais elle fait plus encore: car c'est elle qui prête à la Logique les *formes* rigoureuses et précises qui doivent la rendre infaillible." Leibniz' Universal Characteristic (cf. *ibid.*, chap. iv) realizes "the ideal of formal Logic"; "c'est en elle que la Logique et la Mathématique s'unissent, s'entr'aident et se confondent."

88. Cf. his second letter to Clarke § 1, *loc. cit.*, p. 15; also *G.*, VII, p. 299. The latter passage contains what is perhaps Leibniz' most exhaustive statement of the principle of non-contradiction (identity), and shows that he also regarded the law of excluded middle as part of it, or involved in it.

89. See, e.g., *O. F.*, p. 186; *N. E.*, IV, x, §§ 2-4.

90. *O. F.* p. 371. See also *G.*, III, p. 259: The "ultimate analysis of all necessary truth" is into "definitions or ideas, and identical truths or the coincidence of ideas. And all necessary truths are virtually identical."

91. Second letter to Clarke (1715), § 1, *loc. cit.*, p. 15.

92. *N. E.*, IV, ii, §§ 9-12.

93. Letter to Simon Foucher, *G.*, I, p. 369. (Gerhardt gives 1676 as the date of this letter, but the most recent edition of Leibniz' correspondence (by the Prussian Academy) corrects this to 1675 [see Leroy Loemker, *Gottfried Wilhelm von Leibniz: Philosophical Papers and Letters* (Chicago: University of Chicago Press, 1956), vol. I, p. 566, n. 131].)

94. See, e.g., second letter to Clarke, pp. 15-16; *T.*, p. 45; *O.F.*, pp. 18-20. See also Leroy Loemker, "Leibniz's Judgements of Fact," *Journal of the History of Ideas*, vol. VII (1946), esp. pp. 402-409.

95. The first section of the second letter to Clark (*loc. cit.*) can be read as implying that *only* logic and mathematics consist of necessary truths. In an undated paper (*G.*, VII, p. 301) he seems to indicate that the principle of identity alone is not sufficient for establishing *at least* "a large part" of metaphysics, theology, and ethics, as well as physics. As these passages show, "demonstrable" and "necessary" are not equivalent terms in Leibniz' later philosophy, since he maintains that some contingent truths may be demonstrated a priori by the principle of sufficient reason. Therefore, the fact that he says in the *Nouveaux*

Essais that "part" of morality is demonstrable does not in itself establish that he believes ethical truths to be necessary. (Cf. *N.E.*, III, ii, §§ 11-21; IV, iii, § 19.) This observation also applies to the metaphysical and physical principles listed as "demonstrable" at *N.E.*, IV, iii, § 18. It is true, however, that even in as late a work as the *Nouveaux Essais* Leibniz shows some tendency to compare ethics and metaphysics with mathematics: cf. II, xxix, § 12; I, ii, § 9. In the first passage of these two, on the other hand, the view that ethics and metaphysics may be expounded with "mathematical rigor" is advanced in what anyone familiar with Leibniz' normal idiom could only regard as notably cautious and hesitant terms.

96. An exception to this rule are the "disparates" ("yellowness is not sweetness") and incompatibles ("what is white is not black") to be discussed in chapter iii. These, however, Leibniz explicitly admits as necessary *in loco*.

97. "I admit that the scholastic form of argument is ordinarily inconvenient, insufficient, badly managed, but I say at the same time, that nothing could be more important than the art of formal argument according to the true Logic." (*N.E.* IV, xvii, §4.)

CHAPTER II

SEVENTEENTH CENTURY OPPOSITION: THE INTUITIONISM OF DESCARTES AND LOCKE

Consideration of the views of Descartes and Locke is important for an understanding of Leibniz' doctrine of necessary truth because of the extent to which he defined and justified his own doctrine in relation to their opposing positions. It is not, of course, the case that Descartes and Locke developed *their* views in opposition to Leibniz' position, *per se*. They did, however, proceed in conscious and deliberate opposition to scholastic and formalistic doctrines which we have seen to be the basis of Leibniz' theory. The relevant points of their position for the present discussion are chiefly the following. They maintain, (a) that there are many "self-evident" truths, including a large number of mathematical propositions; (b) that reduction of one self-evident truth to another is a complete waste of time, in as much as there is no more perfect certainty than intuitive self-evidence; (c) that even in the many cases where demonstration is necessary if we are to become assured of the truth or falsity of a proposition, this demonstration should properly take the form of a "chain of intuitions," rather than a chain of definitions.[1]

1. DESCARTES

Descartes stigmatizes reliance on formal demonstration or calculation as opening the door to sophistry and error, and argues that the establishment of conclusions by mere manipulation of a formal calculus, exclusive of intuition, is a "blind" process which precludes a real understanding of the truths arrived at.[2] He is particularly contemptuous of the traditional preoccupation with definition,[3] and, in a well-known letter to Clerselier, is expressly scornful of the notion that the principle of non-contradiction should be regarded as a first principle, to which other propositions are to be reduced:

> That *it is impossible one and the same thing should at one and the same time both be and not be* is a principle [in one sense of the term] and . . . in general it can serve, not properly for the obtaining of knowledge of the existence of anything, but solely, once we know it to exist, in confirming the truth of its existence, by a reasoning such as the following: it is impossible that what is should not be; now I know that such a thing is: therefore I know that it is impossible that it should not be. This is quite unimportant, and makes us no wiser . . .
>
> I further add that we should not require of [a] first principle that it be such that all other propositions be reducible to and be proved by it . . . For it may be that there is in the world no one single first principle to which all things can be reduced.
>
> The reduction of other propositions to the principle, *it is impossible that one and the same thing should at one and the same time both be and not be*, is a manner of reasoning which is superfluous and useless . . . [4]

Of course it is easy to agree that employment of the principle in the way illustrated by Descartes in this passage is indeed "a manner of reasoning which is superfluous and useless." The passage may thus perhaps be taken as negative evidence for the point advanced in the last chapter that up till the time of Leibniz the Scholastic doctrine of primacy of the principle of non-contradiction had not been developed in any fruitful or significant way. Descartes' impatience with the Scholastic insistence upon definition must similarly be understood as a reaction against a doctrine which, for all its pretensions, had yet failed to yield valuable scientific or philosophic results.

Certainty and self-evidence.--Descartes was very little concerned with the problem of necessary truth as such; what is rather emphasized throughout his writings is the problem of certainty or self-evidence. Certainty is to be achieved by conscientious employment of the Cartesian method, which accords a basic and central role to "intuition" or "the natural light of the understanding." The latter is explicitly contrasted to formal syllogistic reasoning in the *Regulae ad directionem ingenii*:

> Because, as we have often taught, the forms of the syllogism are of no assistance for perceiving the truth of things, it will profit the reader if he rejects these altogether, and conceives all knowledge whatsoever, which is not derived from the simple and pure intuition of one solitary thing, to be derived through the comparison of two things or more with each other .... When [this operation] is open and simple, no help from art is required for intuiting the truth which it yields, but only the light of nature.[5]

In seeking firmly established knowledge we begin with the intuition of "primary and self-evident principles" and proceed to other principles by a series of self-evident inferences or "deductions."[6] Descartes thus says that there are two "modes" of knowledge--intuition (of self-evident truths) and deduction[7]--but deduction is itself constituted of a series of intuitions.

Primary truths.--Since Descartes does insist (at least in his early writings) on the importance of beginning with simple truths and proceeding from them to the more complex ones, it cannot be said without qualification that he is opposed to the geometrical ideal of reduction. He is, however, firmly opposed to the ideal of *formal* reduction--demonstration by reduction to formal axioms by the substitution of definitions. He appears to have, moreover, a rather generous conception of the number of truths to be admitted as primitive. Although he may have believed the number to be limited, he clearly did not wish to commit himself to the view that it was particularly small. There is, it is true, one passage which appears to contradict this point. In the *Regulae* he writes:

> There are only a few pure and simple natures which, existing primary and *per se*, do not depend on any others, but may be intuited in direct experience, or by some light that is in us; and

> these we say should be carefully observed: for they are the ones which we have called the simplest in any series. All others can only be perceived in so far as they are deduced from these ...[8]

A few pages earlier, however, he has rather emphasized the manifoldness of the first truths:

> By intuition I mean ... the undoubting [non dubium] conception of a clear and attentive mind, which arises from the light of reason alone.... Thus anyone can mentally intuit that he exists, that he thinks, that a triangle is bounded by three lines, a sphere by one superficies, and similar [truths], which are much more numerous than many people think, because they disdain to turn their mind to such simple matters.[9]

In a later work, the *Principia Philosophiae*, he lists as axioms (which may clearly and distinctly be perceived to be true): the principle of non-contradiction ("It is impossible for the same thing to be and not be at the same time"), "What is done cannot be undone," "Whatever thinks must exist while it is thinking"; and adds that there are "innumerable others, which it would not be easy to recount, but which we cannot fail to know, when the occasion occurs to think on them, and we are not blinded by prejudice."[10] It must be mentioned that some of Descartes' primitive truths--e.g., "I exist"--are treated by Leibniz as contingent, and hence as not reducible to the principle of identity.[11] However, there can be no question that Descartes, particularly in his later works, allows a rather wide scope to intuition. It is evident from the *Meditations*, moreover, that Descartes was prepared to count at least elementary arithmetical propositions, such as "$2 + 3 = 5$", among the "simplest and most manifest" truths;[12] and this represents a sharp point of conflict with Leibniz. Although Descartes did regard the principle of non-contradiction as self-evident, there is no indication that he regarded it as being in any sense prior to elementary truths of mathematics (for instance).

It is further clear from all Descartes' writings, and especially from the *Principia*, that he was not prepared to provide any general characterization of the primitive truths--let alone any formal conditions of primitiveness--beyond the statement that they are such as can be directly perceived to be true. He is content with saying that we "cannot fail to know them" when we happen to think of them. In an earlier part of the *Principia*, however, he notes that others "have admitted as very certain and self-evident [principles] which seem to us to be false."[13]

Although, as far as I have been able to discover, Descartes himself does not expressly make this point, it would appear to follow from his principles-- particularly as stated in his later works, where he places less emphasis on reduction to simples--that demonstration is valuable only in so far as it is subjectively felt to be necessary. But if this is the case, one might well find fault with Euclid for providing *too many* demonstrations--i.e., for offering demonstrations of propositions which are already self-evident, or which the natural light reveals to be true. This conclusion was, at any rate, drawn by Arnauld in the *Port Royal Logic*: he cites as one of several major faults of the geometers the fact that they "prove things which do not need to be proved."[14] The extent to which Arnauld is influenced by Descartes in presenting this objection is fully indicated by his further comment:

> this fault is no doubt a result of not having considered that all the certitude and evidence of our knowledge in the natural sciences comes from this principle: *in respect of anything one may be assured of whatever is contained in a clear and distinct idea*. From which it follows that if we do not need, in order to know that an attribute is included in an idea, anything except the simple consideration of the idea, without adding in any others, that should pass for evident and clear . . . .[15]

Thus, as Leibniz observes critically in the *Nouveaux Essais*, Arnauld actually assumes more axioms than Euclid, and regards it as meritorious to have done so.[16] Opposition to reductionism as an ideal, while not explicitly present in Descartes' writings (except in a qualified form, as in the letter to Clerselier), must, nevertheless, be regarded as a natural consequence of exalting "self-evidence" as a criterion of truth, and of refusing to place any definite restriction on the number of primitives.

Necessity.--I have observed that Descartes is not centrally concerned with the problem of necessity. But he does assert in the *Regulae* (an early work) that the relation discovered by intuition between simple ideas may be either necessary or contingent, and attempts to state what he means by "necessary." Here again, he has recourse to the notion of "distinct conception": the connection is necessary "when one is so implicated in the concept of the other in some confused way, that we cannot conceive either distinctly, if we judge it to be separate from the other."[17] Thus "4 and 3 is 7" is a necessary truth, "for we do not conceive the number seven distinctly, unless we include in it the number three and the number four in some confused way."[18] There are various difficulties with this account, however, of which not the least serious is that the ideas in question are supposed to be "simple."[19] Further, the words "could not" appear in the definition, leaving an impression of emptiness or circularity. Moreover, Descartes elsewhere seems to think that a proposition of which we cannot conceive the opposite could actually be false[20]--a view which would appear to cancel out his account of necessity altogether. It is not surprising, therefore, that Leibniz found little to borrow from in Descartes' remarks on this subject. But his objections to Cartesian intuitionism are predicated on more general and fundamental issues than obscurities in the account of necessary truth.

Leibniz' objection: the need for non-subjective criteria.--To Leibniz, for whom objectivity, and in particular the possibility of resolving disagreements among men, is one of the primary desiderata of any method of establishing truths,[21] Descartes' determination to rely on an essentially subjective power or faculty as the ultimate arbiter in questions of truth and falsity is futile and unscientific. The notion of "clear and distinct conception" which Descartes makes the starting point of his method (and through which he seeks to elucidate the nature of necessity) is according to Leibniz, quite useless as long as we lack a criterion for clarity and distinctness--i.e., a *formal* criterion:

> I postulate therefore palpable criteria of truth, which leave no more doubt than numerical calculi; thus I disregard those criteria, which involve even a little difficulty, as when they

say that that is true which is clearly and distinctly perceived. For there is need of palpable signs [opus est notis palpabilibus] of the clear and the distinct, seeing that men often disagree about them. In the same way I do not approve of building arguments on ideas, since when one person asserts that he finds the attribute which is in question in the idea of the thing, and another maintains the contrary, there is left no way of ending the controversy between them.[22]

Similarly, in his essay criticizing Descartes' *Principia* he remarks:

> Elsewhere I have explained that there is not much use in laying down this rule: that we should only assent to what is clear and distinct, unless better signs are offered of the clear and the distinct than what Descartes gives. The rules of Aristotle and the Geometers are superior: that except for principles (i.e., first truths and hypotheses) we should admit nothing that is not proved by valid argument.[23]

He goes on to explain that he means by "valid argument" one which involves neither a "formal nor a material fallacy." A material fallacy occurs when something is assumed which is not itself a principle and has not been derived from principles by valid argument. By "correct form" he says he understands,

> not only that of common syllogistic, but also any [form] demonstrated beforehand in which the conclusion is dictated by the structure [quae vi suae dispositionis concludit]; which is the case even with the forms of the operations of arithmetic and algebra . . . .[24]

It is not merely a matter of objectivity, moreover. Whereas Descartes believed that formal reasoning encouraged bad thinking by discouraging understanding and attention, Leibniz argues that *inattention to form* is a primary source of error in serious matters,--and elaborates this point with particular reference to Descartes' own mistakes.[25] Further by insisting on an "intuition" at every step, Cartesianism opposed scientific progress by discouraging the development of streamlined algorithms which could render our calculations much more rapid, efficient, and secure.[26]

Leibniz' doctrine of necessary truth must be understood in close connection with his resolute adherence to the formalistic point of view, to which the passages just quoted are adequate testimony. The notion of formal reducibility to identity provides the basis for a general explication of the nature of necessary truth; and at the same time provides a general and objective method of putting the truth of large classes of propositions beyond doubt. Thus Leibniz remarks in a terse note to Principium 50 (in which, as we observed above, Descartes claims that axioms will always be recognized as axioms by anyone whose mind is not clouded by prejudice): "Truths which are quite simple, but which are nevertheless not admitted on account of the prejudiced opinion of men, it is most advisable to demonstrate by simpler ones."[27] Far from abandoning proofs which we have already discovered, as Arnauld advocates and as Descartes' philosophy seems to entail, we must make every effort to secure and systematize knowledge by accepting nothing as primitives except definitions and the principle of identity, and by seeking to demonstrate all other truths by these.[28]

But Leibniz also objects to Cartesian intuitionism on the separate count that in repudiating reduction to the principle of non-contradiction (identity) it throws little or no light on the questions of the nature and grounds of the truth and necessity of mathematical propositions. Thus he writes that Descartes "n'a pas connu la veritable source des vérités."[29] Descartes wants to know (with certainty) *that* a given proposition is true; Leibniz is equally interested in questions of "why" the proposition is true (or necessarily true); in what its truth (or necessity) consists; etc. These interests of Leibniz are, however, brought out most clearly in his replies to the series of arguments presented by Locke in the *Essay* against the validity of the enterprise of reduction. To these we shall now turn.

2. LOCKE

Locke's view of the nature of knowledge is strikingly similar to that of Descartes.[30] He closely parallels Descartes' dictum that (aside from immediate perception of the existence of external objects)[31] knowledge involves the "comparison of two things or more with each other":

> *Knowledge* then seems to me to be nothing but *the perception of the connexion and agreement, or disagreement and repugnancy of any of our ideas.*[32]

> A man is said to know any proposition, which having been laid once before his thoughts, he evidently perceives the agreement or disagreement of the ideas whereof it consists . . . .[33]

And like Descartes he holds that this knowledge may be of two sorts--intuitive and demonstrative.

> If we will reflect on our own ways of thinking we will find, that sometimes the mind perceives the agreement or disagreement of two ideas *immediately by themselves*, without the intervention of any other: and this I think we may call *intuitive knowledge.*[34]

In other cases, however, "the mind cannot so bring its ideas together as by their juxta-position or application one to another, to perceive their agreement or disagreement."[35] In these cases the mind can only discover disagreement or agreement among the ideas in question by use of intervening ideas:

> Those intervening ideas, which serve to show the agreement of any two others, are called *proofs*; and where the agreement and disagreement is by this means plainly and clearly perceived, it is called *demonstration* . . . .[36]

Locke follows Descartes in seeing demonstration as a series of separate intuitions:

> In the next degree of knowledge which I call demonstrative, this intuition is necessary in all the connexions of the

intermediate ideas, without which we cannot attain knowledge and certainty.[37]

Self-evident truths.--Like Descartes, Locke makes little effort to clarify the question of how we are to distinguish intuitable or self-evident[38] truths from propositions which require demonstration, beyond the presentation of examples. Complex geometrical propositions are counted among those only knowable by demonstration: Locke mentions "the three angles of a triangle are equal to two right ones."[39] On the other hand, he is even more emphatic than Descartes in insisting that there is a wide variety of truths subject to immediate or intuitive knowledge. As examples of these he lists the following: various assertions concerning the "identity or diversity" of the mind's ideas, including "particular" propositions such as "a man is a man" and "blue is not yellow," as well as the general principles of identity and contradiction; one truth of "co-existence" ("two bodies cannot be in the same place"); a very large number of particular mathematical truths such as "one and one are equal to two," "three times two are six"; together with the "maxims" of mathematics, such as "equals taken from equals the remainder will be equal";[40] and finally, the fact of our own existence.[41]

From his contention that there are many, many self-evident truths, Locke proceeds to a general attack on the enterprise of reducing all knowledge to one or more "general maxims." I propose to discuss three major points of this polemic, which bear particularly on Leibniz' doctrine, and which have to do with (1) the relation of maxims to their instances; (2) the absurdity of attempting to prove a truth which is already certain; and (3) the triviality of identities and definitional statements.

The relation of maxims to their instances.--Locke maintains that a particular truth is in no sense less evident than the general maxim of which it is an instance. "Equals taken from equals, the remainder will be equal" has "no clearer self-evidence" than the following particular instance of it: "if you take from the five fingers of the one hand two, and from the five of the other hand two, the remaining numbers will be equal."[42] Similarly, he claims that both the general maxim "whatsoever is, is" and such instances of it as "a man is a man" are perfectly and equally self-evident.

All this Leibniz is able to accept without difficulty, only pausing to point out the superior usefulness, in science, of the more general formulations:

> It is true, and I have already remarked that it is as evident to say ecthetically in particular A is A, as to say in general, something is that which it is.[43]

> As to the axiom of Euclid, applied to the fingers of the hand, I am ready to agree that it is as easy to conceive what you say in respect to the fingers, as to see it in respect to A and B, but in order not to do the same thing often, it we mark it generally and after that it is enough to make subsumptions [il suffit de faire des subsomtions]. Otherwise it would be as if one preferred a calculus of particular numbers to universal rules, which would be to obtain less than one can.[44]

In fact, in the *Nouveaux Essais* and in other writings, Leibniz frequently remarks that the number of primitives will be "infinite," since it will include not only the general formulation of the principle of non-contradiction (identity) but also all particular immediate instances of it, such as "I have written what I have written," "An equilateral rectangle is a rectangle," etc.[45]

Locke, however, wishes to go further than this. He wants to deny that what he himself calls the particular "instances" of maxims are in any sense dependent on the maxims of which they are instances. Maxims and instances are, on his view, separate truths, apprehended separately and with no intrinsic relation to each other. He appears to hold, moreover, that if any relationship of priority is to be allowed between the two classes of propositions, the instances must be regarded as prior to the maxims; since particular ideas are apprehended by the individual earlier than general ideas, with the result that a person is aware that a man is a man, for instance, well before he is ready to bear witness to the fact that everything is identical with itself:

> Cannot a country wench know that, having received a shilling from one that owes her three, and a shilling also from another that owes her three, the remaining debts in each of their hands are equal? Cannot she know this, I say, unless she fetch the

certainty of it from this maxim, that if you take equals from equals, the remainder will be equals, a maxim which possibly she never heard or thought of? I desire any one to consider, from what has been elsewhere said, which is known first and clearest by most people, the particular instance, or the general rule; and which it is that gives life and birth to the other.[46]

The first contention--that "a man is a man," "white is white," etc.; and the general "maxim" of identity, are all independent truths, separately established by the individual by a comparison of the ideas involved in each case--is important in the present context because it appears to constitute a challenge to Leibniz' view that all identicals are true in virtue of the principle of identity. Locke's formulation of his position is as follows:

> Whenever the mind with attention considers any proposition, so as to perceive two ideas signified by the terms, and affirmed or denied one of the other to be the same or different; it is presently and infallibly certain of the truth of such a proposition; and this equally whether these propositions be in terms standing for more general ideas, or such as are less so: v.g. whether the general idea of Being be affirmed of itself, as in this proposition, 'whatsoever is, is'; or a more particular idea be affirmed of itself, as 'a man is a man'; or 'whatever is white is white . . . .[47]

This assertion may be supposed to represent the extreme of anti-formalism. Locke is here contending that a separate intuition of the 'sameness' of the ideas that constitute for him the meaning of the terms of a proposition is necessary to establish the truth of each of the infinite number of identicals. His view has, moreover, the curious result that particular identicals are really no more "instances" of the principle of identity than, say "cerulean is cerulean" is an instance of "blue is blue." (I.e., the relation of instance to maxim is reduced to a matter of the extension of a more "particular" term being comprehended in that of a more general term: all ideas fall under the *summum genus* of "being.")

Leibniz replies by simply denying that maxims and their instances may be regarded as separate truths:

> To say that the body is larger than the trunk, does not differ from the axiom of Euclid [that a whole is greater than its parts], except in that this axiom is limited to what is essential [se borne à ce qu'il faut précisement]: but in exemplifying it and giving it body, one makes the intelligible sensible, because to say that a certain whole is larger than a certain one of its parts is in effect the proposition that a whole is larger than its parts, but with the features charged with a certain coloring or addition; as when someone says AB, he says A. Thus one must not oppose here the axiom and the example as different truths in this respect, but consider the axiom as incorporated in the example and rendering the example true.[48]

In maintaining that the maxim and its instances are "different truths" Locke apparently has in mind the fact that the one can "know" that a man is a man, although one has "never heard or thought of" the principle of identity. But Leibniz argues that his point is irrelevant: the axiom is "incorporated" in its instance, whether explicitly recognized or not. Further, if the fact that the instance is "thought of" before the maxim does not establish that they are essentially "different truths," it *a fortiori* fails to establish that the particular instance "gives life and birth" to the maxim. It is, in fact, unclear what Locke could mean by the latter assertion. Leibniz takes him to be implying that maxims are known only by induction from their instances;[49] but as far as I can see this interpretation is not justified by anything that Locke says, and it is quite inconsistent with his express position that maxims, like instances, are apprehended by direct comparison of the ideas involved. It is more likely that what Locke has in mind is that apprehension of maxims involving general ideas presupposes possession of the particular ideas involved in the "instances" of maxims; since on his view general ideas are derived by "abstraction" from particulars: though this does not really entail that maxims depend on their instances, unless he also wishes to maintain that the ability to *compare* general ideas is somehow dependent on the ability to *compare* particular ideas (which does not appear from the text).

Different conceptions of a principle.--It will now be evident that Locke and Leibniz are divided by radically different conceptions of the nature of a principle. For Locke, a principle is something generated by the comparison of ideas, and dependent for its character on the character of the ideas compared. Locke would thus regard it as nonsense to say that two statements involving different ideas could be "true by the same principle." Similarly, he would regard the suggestion that "a man is a man" *incorporates* the principle of identity as nonsensical on the grounds that since the two propositions involve different ideas they are necessarily different and independent. For Leibniz, on the other hand, a principle may be given independently of any specific ideas: it exists, as it were, "above the level" of ideas,[50] so that it is perfectly intelligible to speak of "substituting different ideas in the same principle," and hence to speak of two different statements being true by the same principle. A principle is a matter of the "configurations" of ideas and not of their character:

> Whoever knows that ten is more than nine, that the body is larger than the finger, and that a house is too large to escape out the door, knows each of these particular propositions by the same general reason, which is, as it were, incorporated and colored in the particular [par une même raison génerale qui y est comme incorporée et enluminée], just as one sees features charged with colors, where the proposition and configuration are properly constituted of the features, whatever the color may be [consiste proprement dans les traits, quelle que soit la couleur].[51]

The well-known fact that Locke and Leibniz have different conceptions of what it is for one truth to depend on, or be derived from, or be grounded in another, can actually be seen as a consequence of their different conceptions of the nature of a principle. Leibniz seems to suggest that Locke has simply misconceived or misunderstood what is really at stake:

> It is not a question here of the history of our discoveries, which is different for different men, but of the connection and natural order of truths [de la liaison et de l'ordre naturel des veritez], which is always the same.[52]

The fact that a person may be aware of the truth that "a man is a man" before he has ever thought or heard of the principle of identity is completely irrelevant, according to Leibniz, to the question of which *proposition* should be regarded as prior to the other. The latter question must be understood as having to do with the relation of *logical* (or as Leibniz rather puts it, *natural*) priority. This notion of natural priority, however, Leibniz does not elucidate otherwise than by repeatedly insisting (as in passages already quoted) that a general maxim is naturally prior to its particular instances; and also to whatever truths may be derived from it by the substitution of definitions.

What Leibniz fails to observe is that there is simply no room in Locke's philosophy for the notion of a logical or "natural" order of truths as Leibniz understands it. It is not the case that Locke merely overlooks the fact that a formal, and not a psychological relation among propositions is in question. Rather Locke, following Descartes, has resolutely turned his back on the whole notion of a formal order. There is no aspect of a proposition which is in any way independent of the character of the ideas involved:[53] i.e., there is no isolable formal aspect which it is the purpose of a general axiom to express. The general axiom must be regarded, according to Locke, as a separate and independent truth, and not as the expression of a form shared by many truths, as the notion of an instance seems to require. The notion of a logically derivative truth is similarly excluded, since like the notion of an instance, it assumes the intelligibility of substituting different "ideas" in the same principle.

This is not to say that "derivation" of one truth from another can have no sense for Locke, but that it can have *only* a psychological sense. Thus we are able to achieve certainty of many geometrical truths, only by first perceiving "the immediate agreement of the intervening ideas, whereby the agreement or disagreement of the two ideas under examination (whereof the one is always the first, the latter the last in the account) is found."[54] This is to say that in order to apprehend the truth of "the square of the hypotenuse of a right triangle is equal to the sum of the squares of the two sides," we must discover whether the subject idea (denoted by "the square . . . triangle"), is the same as the predicate idea (denoted by "the sum . . . sides"), and to make this discovery we will have to employ further propositions asserting the agreement of "intervening ideas."[55] The conclusion may be regarded as deriving from assertions of agreement between intervening ideas, just in so far as our perception of the truth of the conclusion depends on our perception of the truth of intervening statements: i.e. strictly in so far as our certain knowledge of the one derives from our certain knowledge of the others. It is in this sense that Locke may speak of a "clear and fit order" among truths, in which they should be laid out "to make their connexion and force be plainly and easily perceived"; and of "the dependence of the conclusion on all the parts."[56]

Necessary truths which are not expressly identical: self-evident or derivative?--The issues at stake between Locke and Leibniz become more complicated when we turn to propositions which while necessary (according to both of them) are not express identities (immediate instances of identical maxims). For, while Leibniz is prepared to agree that immediate instances are as evident as maxims of which they *are* immediate instances (i.e. that the particular is not necessarily less evident than the general), he apparently wishes to hold that all necessary truths which are not express identities are less evident and certain than express identities. He writes, for instance, that identities and the principle of contradiction are the only non-contingent truths that one cannot "revoquer en doute";[57] or that cannot be proved by something "more certain":[58] they alone are "incontestable".[59] Locke, in opposition, vigorously maintains that we are as certain of the truth of, e.g., such elementary arithmetical propositions as "two and two are four", "three times two are six", as we are of *any* proposition:

> Many a one knows that one and two are equal to three, without having heard, or thought on . . . any . . . axiom by which it might be proved; and knows it as certainly as any other man knows, that 'the whole is equal to all its parts,' or any other

> maxim; and all from the same reason of self-evidence: the equality of those ideas being as visible and certain to him without that or any other axiom as with it . . . . . . What principle is requisite to prove that one and one are two, that two and two are four, that three times two are six? . . . To which, if we add all the self-evident propositions which may be made about all our distinct ideas, principles will be almost infinite . . . .[60]

Hence, Locke says, the notion that such a proposition as "two and two are four" needs proof "takes away the foundations of all knowledge and certainty," since if one part of self-evident knowledge needs proof, so will every other.[61]

One may well wonder how this dispute is to be decided. Are express identities, or are they not, the only self-evident non-contingent[62] truths. Leibniz offers in justification of his position only such dogmatic assertions as: "It is absolutely impossible that there be truths of reason [non-contingent truths] as evident as the identicals or immediates."[63] But in what sense is it "absolutely impossible"? What justification can there be for regarding "identical" and "immediate" as equivalent, beyond the *preconception* that all and only express identities are self-evident? But if we turn to Locke we find merely the equally dogmatic assertion that elementary arithmetical truths *are* as evident as identities (or the injunction to consult our natural light and *see* if they are not as evident). Must we regard this as simply an ultimate incompatibility of intuitions--Locke's natural light yielding one result and Leibniz' another?

It is hard to escape the conclusion that if the question of exclusive primacy of the principle of non-contradiction--or its status as the ground or foundation of other truths--is to be decided on grounds of self-evidence, and if "self-evidence" means something like "perfect and unconditional certainty of the truth of a given proposition," Locke is standing on firm ground in denying the exclusive primacy of this principle. Can it really be denied that we are as certain that two and two are four as we are that two is equal to two? Can it really be maintained that a theoretical proof such as the one Leibniz offers in the *Nouveaux Essais*[64] of "2+2=4" can make us *more certain* of the truth of this proposition?

It might be suggested that Leibniz' doctrine of necessity does not strictly require that the self-evidence of the principle of non-contradiction be *the grounds of our certainty* of all necessary truths. It is the grounds of their *necessity*, and is the primary principle in this sense; moreover, it may be the case that to see that a proposition is necessary is to see that it is certain. But is it not consistent with all this to admit that we may be perfectly certain of the truth of a proposition completely independently of any apprehension of the "grounds of its necessity"? But then why does Leibniz find it necessary to contend that the principle of identity and its instances are prior in certainty and self-evidence to all other propositions--when this contention seems in itself so highly dubious? Why can he not simply accept Locke's point that in a sense there are many "first truths of reason" besides identity--i.e. there are many propositions of which we are as certain as we can be, independently of any "proof" of their truth?

It must be acknowledged that there are times when Leibniz *does* seem implicitly to be accepting Locke's point. In a letter to Jean Bernouilli (who had inquired whether he wished to call into question the axiom "the whole is larger than the part") Leibniz argues for a distinction between requesting a demonstration of an axiom and feeling doubt about its truth.[65] It is also worth noting in this connection the manner in which Leibniz introduces his well-known proof of the proposition "2+2=4". Locke's advocate Philalethis demands to know what principle is needed "to prove that two and two are four"--claiming, after Locke, that the truth of such propositions is known "without the aid of any proof." It is significant that Leibniz in replying to this point does not dispute the contention that "2+2=4" is perfectly well-known to be true without proof. Instead, he denies that it is an *immediate* truth--and not on the grounds that it "requires" proof in some psychological sense, but on the grounds that it is susceptible of reduction:

> I am well prepared for that question. That two and two are four is not a completely immediate truth [une verité tout à fait

immediate]. Suppose that four signifies three and one. It can then be demonstrated; and I shall show you how . . . .[66]

Having completed the proof, he puts into Philalethis' mouth the following words:

> This demonstration, *as little necessary as it may be with respect to its well-known conclusion* [quelque peu necessaire qu'elle soit par rapport à sa conclusion trop connue], serves to show how truths depend on definitions and Axioms [ont de la dependance des definitions et des Axiomes.][67] (my emphasis)

Such passages as this give further indication of the extent to which Leibniz was preoccupied with the logical or "natural" order which he believed to obtain among propositions themselves, as opposed to the chronological order in which a given individual happens to apprehend the propositions as true. Reduction to identity is a worthwhile undertaking regardless of whether the proposition to be reduced "needs proof" in the ordinary sense, since it is only through reduction that this logical or natural order can be brought to light. By the same token, it is intrinsically worthwhile to make clear the grounds of the necessity of a proposition whether its truth is really in question or not. Thus Leibniz writes that, aside from the question of whether or not we may be confident of the truth of the undemonstrated geometrical axiom, if we should forego reduction,

> We would be deprived of what I most esteem in geometry, in respect to contemplation [par rapport à la contemplation], which is the disclosure of the real source of eternal truths and of the way of enabling us to understand this necessity [du moyen de nous en faire comprendre la necessité] . . . .[68]

In spite of his insistence on the distinction between the logical order of truths and the chronological order in which they are apprehended by individuals, however, Leibniz is not in the last analysis prepared to concede that we may achieve perfect certainty of a necessary truth without any reference to its logical grounds in identity. He has two rather different ways of supporting this position against Locke's contention that many arithmetical and geometrical truths are evident to us prior to any consideration or employment of "maxims". The one I will consider first involves a revision of the ordinary conception of "perceiving the logical grounds" of a truth; the second centers on the notion of a proposition's being perfectly certain.

The first defense of the view that our certain apprehension of truths of reason always involves the principle of identity turns on the conception of unconscious or "implicit" employment of a maxim. Thus, in several passages of the *Nouveaux Essais* we find the suggestion that the fact that an elementary truth of arithmetic (for example) is apprehended and maintained by an individual before he has ever heard of the principle of identity does not establish that the former is known independently of the latter. In the case of necessary truths, certainty always derives from perception of the fact that the ideas involved are related by identity--although this perception need not be "explicit" or conscious:

> If the truths are quite simple and evident, and quite close to the identities and definitions, one hardly needs to employ the Maxims expressly in order to draw these truths from them, since the mind employs them implicitly [virtuellement] and draws its conclusion at a stroke without any intermediate step [fait sa conclusion tout d'un coup sans entrepos].[69]

In the same vein, he elsewhere likens the implicit employment of maxims in reasoning to the omission of a premise in enthymematic reasoning:

> One founds one's thinking on these general maxims [on se fond sur ces maximes generales], just as one does on the major premises which one suppresses when reasoning by enthememes; for although one often does not pay distinct attention to [ne pense pas distinctement à] what one does in reasoning, any more than to what one does in walking and jumping; it is still true that the force of the conclusion consists partly in what one suppresses [consiste en partie dans ce qu'on suprime] and could not come from anywhere else, as one will find when one wishes to justify it.[70]

Leibniz is unquestionably arguing in both these passages that if the principle of identity is the logical ground of other necessary truths, our certainty of these truths *must* be in some sense derivative from a knowledge of the principle. Since we are, as he admits, not employing it consciously, we *must* be employing it "implicitly" or "virtually." In order to do this we must in a sense know the principle of identity prior to knowing the truths that depend on it.[71] Leibniz, that is, argues from the fact that the principle of identity is the logical grounds of all necessary truths to the contention that it must be in some sense the psychological grounds of our certainty of all these truths ("l'espirt les employe virtuellement"). But one does not have to accept Locke's repudiation of the conception of a logical foundation to find fault with this reasoning. It seems no less paradoxical to suppose that we *unconsciously* carry out the sort of theoretical deduction that Leibniz offers before we are certain that two and two are four, than to suppose that we do so consciously. The enthymeme analogy, at any rate, is of little help. A person reasoning in enthymemes is conscious that he is drawing a conclusion, and makes some of his premises explicit; whereas whether we apprehend "2+2=4" as a conclusion from another truth is precisely what is in question. Moreover, the criterion of a person's having a suppressed premise "implicitly in mind" appears to be that he is able to produce this premise when challenged. We are *not* ready to say, every time someone leaves out a step in reasoning, that his mind has supplied the premise "implicitly." The supposed fact that "2+2=4" may be shown to follow logically from the principle of identity would seem no more to establish that every one who is certain of this truth has (consciously or unconsciously) derived it from identity by the manipulation of definitions, than the fact that "this man is rational" follows from "all men are rational" establishes that I have arrived at certainty of the former proposition by at least "implicitly" carrying out the instantiation. Leibniz seems to assume that if a proposition is logically "justifiable", the mind which is certain of the truth of this proposition must be in some sense in possession of the logical justification; by why should we accept this assumption?

It seems unfortunate that Leibniz, instead of resorting to the intrinsically unverifiable notion of unconscious employment of maxims, does not rest his case for the value of reduction on his own enlightened distinction between psychological and logical order.[72] To discover the "logical ground" of mathematical truths by deriving them from a general logical principle need not increase our certainty of these truths in order to be interesting and scientifically valuable. If the suggestion that we might possibly feel absolutely certain of a truth without having in any sense "perceived its logical grounds" is thought inevitably to lead to a loss of scientific objectivity by admitting subjective certainty as a standard of truth, the issue has simply been misconceived. For a distinction must be recognized between scientific standards and subjective fact.[73] Leibniz himself, indeed, seems to recognize this distinction in at least one place, where he allows that "imagination derived from sense experience" will not permit us to represent to ourselves more than one meeting of two straight lines. He then continues:

> But it is not this on which science should be founded [ce n'est pas sur quoi la science doit être fondée]. And if someone thinks that this act of imagination [cette imagination] gives the connection of distinct ideas, he is not sufficiently instructed in the source of truths, and many propositions that are demonstrable by other prior ones will pass with him for immediate.[74]

We may base our conviction of a truth on "imagination": *mais ce n'est pas sur quoi la science doit être fondée*. Surely it is sufficient for Leibniz' purposes of repudiating the Cartesian methodology to draw this line between the subjective and the scientifically admissable or interesting, and to place "intuitions" in the former category, admitting only reasoning set forth with the greatest possible formal exactitude in the latter. The attempt to establish that subjective processes fundamentally conform to our standards of objectivity is as unnecessary as it is implausible.

Leibniz does have a second way of arguing for the view that the principle of identity must be regarded as prior to all other non-contingent truths not only in respect of logical order, but also in respect of our certain knowledge. This second approach is already suggested in the passage just quoted. It makes no essential use of the notion of the implicit employment of maxims, but rather turns on the distinction between a "distinct" and a "confused" perception of the connection between ideas:

> To doubt seriously is to doubt with respect to practice [douter par rapport à la pratique]. And certainty may be taken to be a knowledge of truth, with which one cannot doubt with respect to practice without folly ... But Evidence is a luminous certainty [une certitude lumineuse], that is, a case where one does not doubt because of the connection that one sees among ideas [à cause de la liaison qu'on voit entre les idées].[75]

Clarity and evidence should therefore be regarded as "une espece de la certitude." "Evidence" is absent as long as the true connection between the "ideas" of a proposition is not clearly and precisely apprehended: it will therefore be absent, in the case of a necessary truth, as long as the reducibility of the proposition to identity is not apprehended. *For as long as one has not seen that the proposition is reducible to identity one has not seen the real grounds of the connection of the ideas.* Thus, one may be very certain indeed of the truth of such a proposition prior to demonstration, but one's certainty will not at this point be "luminous": one's perception of the truth will be in some sense confused, as long as the connection of the ideas by identity has not actually been exhibited:

> What you have said [Monsieur] ... concerning the connection of ideas as the real source of truths requires explication. If you wish to be satisfied with seeing this connection in a confused way, you will weaken the exactitude of demonstrations .... But if you wish this connection of ideas to be seen and expressed distinctly, you will be obliged to have recourse to Definitions and identical Axioms.[76]

It should be quite obvious to us (although it apparently was not to Leibniz) that Locke could never accept this understanding of "self-evidence," since he allows no room for the notion of logical foundation on which it depends. For this reason, Locke could not and would not admit that we arrive at a more distinct or "luminous" apprehension of the connection between ideas when we have carried out a formal reduction to identity. For Locke, the true connection between ideas is exactly what we apprehend it to be by our intuition, and not something that is formally expressible. Whereas formal demonstration is regarded by Leibniz as producing a more "luminous" certainty of truths which we may have felt quite certain of prior to demonstration, it would be regarded by Locke as introducing confusion and complexity into what is already perfectly clear and simple.

But what must be observed is that, in the light in which it is now set, the issue between Locke and Leibniz can no longer be thought of as one that might or that must be decidable by simple introspection. Leibniz does not seem to be saying that we must be *aware* that our conception of the truth of "2+2=4" is confused before we have seen it demonstrated: we do not need to *feel* confused or doubtful about the truth of the proposition. By the same token, once the matter has been put on this ground, the fact that "2+2=4" does not seem to *need* proof, or even to be rendered more certain by proof, no longer provides the basis for an objection to Leibniz' position concerning the primacy of the principle of identity. For "luminous certainty" has come (virtually by definition) to signify *the state of mind in which the logical grounds of an arithmetical or other necessary truth are apprehended*. The criterion by which one identifies "evidence" or "luminous certainty" is the possession or perception of the "logical grounds" of a necessary truth (which is also the ground of its necessity). Leibniz is saying that this state of mind is the one which, as scientists, we should try to arrive at. Which is no more than to say that as scientists we should strive to carry out demonstrations of all axioms.

We can now see that the exclusive self-evidence of the principle of identity is not so much an assumption of Leibniz' theory of necessity as a consequence of it (and at the same time a consequence of his formalism, which is inseparable from the doctrine of necessity). It is because Leibniz believes that all necessary truths have their logical foundation in the principle of identity, and that "nothing should be admitted without proof," that he refuses to admit as thoroughly "luminous" any apprehension of these truths which does not see through them to this principle. This is virtually the opposite approach to the Cartesian-Lockean one of consulting our "natural light" to see which truths may be accepted as certain without proof, and seeking demonstrations of the rest. The possession of a proof is the criterion of luminous certainty, according to Leibniz. Whether or not we are (by subjective determination) perfectly certain is the criterion by which to decide whether or not we need a proof, according to Locke (and also Descartes). The scientific method is expounded with reference to "self-evidence" by the Cartesians; "self-evidence" is interpreted in terms of his ideal of objective science by Leibniz. The possibility of admitting the principle of identity as the logical foundation of all necessary truths is ruled out *ab initio* by Locke when he refuses to admit into his philosophy the conception of a purely logical or formal relation among truths, independent of the content of the ideas involved. The possibility of admitting that it is not the psychological ground of everyone's perfect certainty of necessary truths is not really seriously considered on its own merits by Leibniz. Instead, he either declares that since it is the logical ground or "source", it must be implicitly the psychological ground or source of certainty; or argues from its being the ultimate logical basis of the relation of ideas in certain propositions to the defectiveness of any apprehension of the relation of these ideas which does not see them as related by this principle. Locke's extreme of denying that "a man is a man" is a consequence of the principle of identity is counterbalanced by Leibniz' extreme of affirming that our minds must be supposed to employ "maxims" implicitly when they cannot be found to do so consciously.

Considering these radical differences in point of view and underlying assumptions from which Locke attacks, and Leibniz defends, the enterprise of reducing mathematical truths to identity, there is no simple way of deciding which side of the issue is the more successfully championed. We have seen, at any rate, that one's answer to the question of whether or not, e.g., elementary arithmetical truths are to be regarded as "self-evident" may substantially depend on the general philosophical outlook with which one begins one's inquiry. If one is centrally concerned with personal certainty, the enterprise of "proving" that two and two are four may well seem pedantic and otiose. If one is convinced at the outset of the importance of formal proof, one will find it easy to deny that there can be "evident knowledge" in the absence of such proof: the certainty of one or many individuals will be taken as quite irrelevant. This is not to deny that strong points may be made on one side or the other which may be regarded as casting doubt on the reasonableness of the opposite position. Thus, there seems to be considerable force in Leibniz' objection that intuition may yield false results: it might be regarded as intuitively obvious, for instance, that two lines which continually approach each other must eventually meet.[77] A Lockean might reply that any logic which yielded the result, "2+2≠4" would be discredited on the basis of this conclusion alone.[78] For the purposes of the present discussion, however, it is enough to be able to conclude that the "intuitionistic" objections of Locke are not decisive against Leibniz' position that all non-contingent truths besides the principle of non-contradiction and express identities are to be regarded as derivative.

The alleged triviality of identities.--Let us now take note of one final point of Locke's: his contention that all identical and all definitional truths, "though they be certainly true, yet they add no light to our understanding, bring no increase to our knowledge," and must hence be regarded as "trifling." In apparent inconsistency with his position, as stated above, that knowledge of identical truths involves the comparison of the ideas involved in each case, Locke here implies that knowledge of the truth of identities amounts to no more or less than knowledge of the *general* truth that a *word* may always be affirmed of itself (and *that* a word may always be affirmed of itself is the whole content and significance of the principle of identity):

> Neither that received maxim ["whatsoever is, is"], nor any other identical proposition, teaches us anything; and though in such kind of propositions this great and magnified maxim, boasted to be the foundation of demonstration, may be and often is made use of to confirm them, yet all it proves amounts to no more than this, That the same word may with great certainty be affirmed of itself, without any doubt of the truth of any such proposition; and let me add also without any real knowledge . . . .
>
> . . . At this rate, any very ignorant person . . . may make a million of propositions of whose truth he may be infallibly

> certain, and yet not know one thing in the world thereby
> ....[79]

Definitional truths, too, such as "every man is an animal," "a palfrey is an ambling horse," teach us nothing but "the signification of words."[80] Locke concludes that there are two sorts of propositions the truth which we can know "with perfect certainty":

> The one is, of those trifling propositions which have a certainty in them but it is only a verbal certainty, but not instructive. And secondly, we can know the truth, and so may be certain in propositions, which affirm something of another, which is a necessary consequence of its precise complex idea, but not contained in it.[81]

As an example of the non-trifling class of certain or necessary truths, Locke offers the geometrical proposition "the external angle of all triangles is bigger than either of the opposite internal angles":

> which relation of the outward angle to either of the opposite internal angles, making no part of the complex idea signified by the name triangle, this is a real truth, and conveys with it an instructive real knowledge.[82]

One may assume, I believe, that Locke would have been prepared to class geometrical and arithmetical truths in general as non-trifling--even those elementary ones which he regarded as self-evident (since these do not, on his view, fall into either the category of identities or of definitional truths).[83]

Setting aside for the time being the question of definition (which will be dealt with in chapter iv), we may consider the relevance of the view that identities are trifling to Leibniz' doctrine. Although the point is not quite explicit in the *Essay*, it seem fairly evident from the passage quoted just above that Locke's *aim* in emphasizing the "uninstructive" character of identities is to discredit the view that they may reasonably be regarded as the "foundation of demonstration" of all necessary and certain knowledge. The observation that identities are "merely trifling" propositions might be supposed to create a strong presumption against the reasonableness of regarding them as the first principles of all demonstration, and in particular against the view that they are the grounds of serious or "instructive" truths of arithmetic and geometry. Other thinkers, at any rate, have accepted as fact the Lockean distinction between trivial and instructive truths, and have taken it to be grounds for dismissing Leibniz' reductionistic position. Russell, for instance, in his *Critical Exposition of the Philosophy of Leibniz*, having observed that for Leibniz all necessary truths are "analytic," comments that the instances which Leibniz gives of "analytic" judgments are either not truly analytic,

> or they are tautologous, and so not properly propositions at all. Thus Leibniz says, on one occasion . . . that primitive truths of reason are identical, because they appear only to repeat the same thing, without giving any information. One wonders, in this case, of what use they can be, and the wonder is only increased by the instances which he proceeds to give. Among these are "A is A," "I shall be what I shall be," "The equilateral rectangle is a rectangle" . . . . Most of these instances assert nothing; the remainder can hardly be considered the foundations of any important truth.[84]

We are meant to conclude with Russell (though not, it is true, on the basis of this argument alone) that the doctrine of the "analyticity" of all necessary truths (and, in particular of the truths of mathematics) is false, if not actually absurd. Similarly, James Gibson observes that Leibniz "entirely failed to grasp" "the significance" of Locke's exposure of the futility" of the effort to reduce necessary truths to identities.[85]

It is, in fact, true that on one level Leibniz' reply seems to miss the point of Locke's remarks on the triviality of the principle of identity. Taking up Locke's statement that the assertion of identical truths is "but like a monkey shifting his oyster from one hand to the other: and [sic] had he but words, might no doubt have said, Oyster in right hand is subject, and oyster in left hand is predicate' . . . ,"[86] he replies:

> I find that this author as full of wit as endowed with judgement has every reason in the world to speak against those

who use [identities] thus. But now you see how one should employ identities to render them useful, i.e., in showing by force of consequences and definitions, that other truths which one wishes to establish reduce to them.[87]

If Locke is taken to be arguing, in the chapter, "Of Trifling Propositions," that identities cannot be the basis of other truths precisely because they are "trifling," Leibniz does in a sense seem to miss Locke's point when he returns that identities are not trifling because they are the basis of other truths. However, two things must be borne in mind. In the first place, Leibniz believes that he has already *shown*, with his proof of "two and two are four" in the previous chapter, that what Locke regards as non-trifling necessary truths *can in fact* be derived from identities; therefore, it is not surprising that he should be unimpressed with general, "a priori" arguments to the effect that express identities cannot conceivably be the basis of demonstrations of other truths. Secondly, Leibniz' suggestion in this reply that the "triviality" (or nontriviality) of a truth is a function of how the truth is used, while perhaps indicative of a superficial reading of Locke, is by no means wholly irrelevant. For it amounts to a disclaimer of Locke's assumption that certain truths have an intrinsic triviality which disqualifies them from serious use. The fact that certain truths are "uninstructive" in Locke's sense, does not entail--Leibniz might wish to argue--that they cannot be put to instructive uses; nor, indeed, that they cannot be the logical basis of truths that we find instructive. Further, if pressed on this point, Leibniz might well point out once more that he is concerned with the logical relations among truths, not with questions of psychology; and that whether or not a given truth is "instructive" is a question of the latter sort. Therefore, he might conclude, the fact that proposition A is "instructive" and proposition B is not, should not create any kind of prejudice about what sort of *logical* relations they may bear to each other. For decisions concerning the logical grounds of various classes of propositions we should turn from intuitionistic preconceptions to serious consideration of the procedure of formal reduction.

Leibniz has, in fact, been partially vindicated, in respect of his position on this point, by subsequent developments in logic and the philosophy of mathematics. Thus, Russell, who in 1900[88] held that tautologies could not even be counted as propositions, and that they could not be considered the foundation of any "important truth," by 1919 is maintaining that all "logical propositions" have "the characteristic . . . we agreed to call "tautology,"[89] and also (on the basis of the achievements in *Principia Mathematica*) that "what can be known, in mathematics and by mathematical methods, is what can be deduced from pure logic."[90] The characteristic, "tautology," which sets off logical truths, is, he remarks, "the one which was felt, and intended to be defined, by those who said that it consisted in deducibility from the law of contradiction"--although Russell denies that the principle of non-contradiction has any "special pre-eminence" among logical truths.[91] Indeed, the present exalted status which Leibniz enjoys as the "founder of mathematical logic"[92] is in part a consequence of his refusal to admit on intuitive Lockean grounds an unbridgeable gap between serious mathematical propositions and the "trivial" logical maxims.

3. CONCLUSION

In this chapter we have seen how Leibniz, profoundly dissatisfied with the intuitionistic reaction against the ideal of formal reduction in his own century, undertook directly to argue against the positions elaborated by Descartes and Locke. In the course of examining Leibniz' opposition to these philosophers, we have seen the extent to which his doctrine of necessary truth is bound up with his ideal of formal proof: reduction to the principle of identity is conceived at once (and with equal importance) as the way of clarifying or explicating the notion of necessity; and of systematizing and revealing the logical foundations of mathematical knowledge--hence reducing error, ignorance, and dispute in this science. I have maintained further that the anti-reductionist arguments elaborated by Locke in the *Essay* do not amount to effective criticism of Leibniz' doctrine. None of this, however, can be construed as constituting a *justification* of Leibniz' theory of necessity. For instance, the question of how far Leibniz was able to go beyond merely *asserting* that all mathematical truths are logically reducible to the principle of identity has not even been raised. This question and others bearing on the cogency of Leibniz' definition of necessary truth will be dealt with in the next chapter.

NOTES

1. Although in the present discussion we shall not deviate from seventeenth century concepts and vocabulary, it is worth noting that criticism of Leibniz' enterprise of formal reduction can be formulated along lines laid out by Descartes and Locke without employing the concepts of intuition or self-evidence. This has been done, for instance, by Keith S. Donnellan (in an unpublished Ph. D. dissertation, "C.I. Lewis and the Foundations of Necessary Truth" [Dept. of Philosophy, Cornell University, 1961]). For the concept of self-evidence Donnellan substitutes notions connected with "knowing a language," etc.

2. See *Regulae ad directionem ingenii*, regulae iv, x; *Discours de la méthode*, ii; *Recherche de la verité*, Adam and Tannery (hereafter "A. & T."), vol. X, p. 522. Also Belaval, *Leibniz critique de Descartes*, esp. chap. i.

3. Regulae x, xii; *Meditationes*, ii (A. & T., vol. xii, p. 25); *Principia philosophiae*, principium x.

4. Letter to Clerselier, June or July, 1646: trans. and quoted by Norman Kemp Smith, *New Studies in the Philosophy of Descartes* (London: Macmillan & Co., 1952), pp. 283-284. The original may be found in vol. VII of Descartes' *Correspondence*, ed. C. Adam and G. Milhaud (Paris: Presses Universitaires de France, 1960), pp. 84-85. Cf. *Recherche de la verité, loc. cit.*

5. Regula XIV, A. & T., vol. X, p. 440.

6. Reg. vii, *ibid.*, pp. 387-388.

7. Reg. iii, *ibid.*, p. 369.

8. Reg. vi, *ibid.*, p. 383.

9. *Ibid.*, p. 368.

10. Principium, i 1 (I)A. & T., vol. VIII, pp. 23-24. Cf. Princ. 1, *ibid.*, p. 24.

11. See below.

12. Cf. Meditatio i, A. & T., vol. VII, p. 21; Med. iii, *ibid.*, pp. 35-36.

13. Princ. v (I), A. & T., vol. VIII, p. 6.
14. *Logique de Port-Royal*, ed. Charles Jourdain (Paris: L. Hachette, 1854), Pt. IV, chap. ix, p. 299. A similar view is expressed by Pascal in "L'Esprit géométrique," which is included in this edition of the *Port Royal Logic*.
15. *Ibid.*, pp. 200-300.
16. *N. E.*, IV, vii, § 1.
17. Reg. xii (A. & T., vol. X, p. 421.)
18. *Ibid.*
19. See Leonard G. Miller, "Descartes, Mathematics, and God" (*Philosophical Review*, LXVI (1957), pp. 451-465) for a thorough and lucid presentation of this and related difficulties in Descartes' conception of necessary truth (esp. pp. 456-57; 459).
20. E.g., *Meditationes*, iii. See Miller, *loc. cit.*, for a more detailed statement of this problem and further references (esp. pp. 452 and 460).
21. Cf. *Log.*, p. 96-97.
22. Quoted by Couturat, *Log.*, pp. 100n. 2, and 203 n. 2. Cf. the long passage quoted above from Arnauld, with reference to "building arguments on ideas."
23. *Animadversiones* . . . , I, ad. artic. 43, 45, 46 (S., p. 31).
24. *Ibid.*
25. See *Animadversiones* . . ., I, ad. artic. 54, 55: "There will be some who read this who will be offended at us for reducing such great philosophers [as Descartes] to the limitations of Scholasticism by putting them in syllogisms; there will perhaps also be those who will condemn this as too trivial. But we have learned that these great philosophers . . . stumble on the most serious matters through neglect of this childish logic; in fact, they scarcely ever make mistakes in any other way. For what else does this logic contain than the most general dictates of supreme reason, expressed in rules that are easy to understand? It has seemed desirable to use [the example just given], to show, for once, how useful such rules are for putting an argument into the prescribed form, so that the force of the argument may

become apparent, especially in problems where the imagination does not come to the aid of reason . . . and where we are dealing with an author [i.e., Descartes] who puts great matters into precipitate arguments." (I have taken this translation from Loemker, vol. II, p. 667)

26. Cf. *Log.*, pp. 95-96.
27. *Animadversiones*, I. ad. artic. 50, (*S.*, p. 32).
28. See, e.g., *N. E.*, *loc. cit.*
29. Letter to Philipp (1679), *G.*, IV, p. 282.
30. It is not important for the purposes of the present discussion that Descartes maintains, and Locke denies, the existence of innate ideas. It will be observed in chap. iv, however, that Leibniz derives some of the arguments he uses against the conventionalist position of Locke and Hobbes from Descartes' doctrine of ideas. Thus it is important not to overemphasize either Locke's acceptance of Cartesian views or Leibniz' rejection of them.
31. John Locke, *An Essay Concerning Human Understanding*, ed. A.C. Fraser (New York: Dover Publications, 1959), Bk. IV, ii, § 14. (The whole of Book IV is contained in the second volume of the two-volume Dover edition.)
32. *Ibid.*, IV, i, § 2.
33. *Ibid.*, § 8.
34. *Ibid.*, ii, § 1.
35. *Ibid.*, § 2.
36. *Ibid.*, § 3.
37. *Ibid.*, § 2.
38. "Where that agreement or disagreement is perceived immediately by itself, without the intervention or help of any other, there our knowledge is self-evident." (*Essay*, IV, vii, § 2.)
39. *Ibid.*, i, § 9.
40. *Ibid.*, vii, §§ 4, 5, 6, 10, etc. In Book I, i, § 16, (Dover ed. vol. I) Locke goes so far as to say: "A man knows that eighteen and nineteen are equal to thirty-seven with the same evidence that he knows one and two to be equal to three . . . ."

41. *Ibid.*, IV, xi, § 2; cf. vii, § 7 (but the phrasing of the point is in the latter passage extremely ambiguous).
42. *Ibid.*, vii, § 6.
43. *N. E.*, IV, vii, §§ 2-4.
44. *Ibid.*, § 6.
45. See, e.g., *O. F.*, p. 186; *N. E.*, IV, vii, § 1.
46. *Essay*;, IV, xii, § 3. See John Yolton, *John Locke and the Way of Ideas* (New York: Oxford University Press, 1956) for information on seventeenth century British proponents of the Scholastic doctrine of the priority of the principle of non-contradiction. It is particularly interesting that at least one man (Sergeant) was maintaining the view that the principles of *identity and non-contradiction* are the first principles of knowledge. (*Ibid.*, pp. 83-84.) Locke appears to have had no close knowledge of the work of Leibniz himself. After the appearance of the *Essay* Leibniz attempted to draw Locke into a direct dialogue concerning the views that were advanced, but his efforts were without avail (cf. the editorial introduction to *N. E.*).
47. *Essay*, IV, vii, § 4.
48. *N. E.*, IV, vii, § 10.
49. *N. E.*, xii, §§ 2-4.
50. Belaval, *Leibniz critique de Descartes*, p. 71.
51. *N. E.*, IV, xii, §§ 1-2.
52. *N. E.*, IV, vii, §§ 8-9. Discrepancies in the spelling of French words which may appear in quotations from the *Nouveaux Essais* are a result of the fact that the edition of this work which is here employed "retains the orthographic diversity of different copyists" (cf. *N. E.*, Introduction, p. xxvi).
53. See in this connection Bk. IV, xii, § 14: "For it being evident that our knowledge cannot exceed our ideas; as far as they are either imperfect, confused, or obscure, we cannot expect to have certain, perfect, or clear knowledge."
54. *Essay*, IV, xi, § 7.
55. Thus, in chapter xvii of Bk. IV Locke speaks repeatedly of the

56. IV, xii, § 3. However, this passage is merely a notable exception to the general rule that Locke almost never speaks explicitly of the "dependence" of one truth on another.
57. *N. E.* I, ii, § 13.
58. *Ibid.,.* IV, ii, § 1.
59. *Ibid.,* I, ii, § 13.
60. *Essay,* IV, vii, § 10.
61. *Essay,* IV, vii, § 19.
62. That Leibniz also admits contingent primary (self-evident) truths will be noted in the next chapter.
63. *N. E.,* I, ii, § 1.
64. *N. E.,* IV, vii, § 10.
65. *Leibnizens mathematische Schriften,* ed. C.J. Gerhardt (Berlin-Halle: Asher and Schmidt, 1849-1863), vol. III, p. 316.
66. *N. E.,* IV, vii, § 10. (Note that Leibniz treats "three and one is four" as a *definition,* not a truth.)
67. *N. E.,* IV, vii, § 10.
68. *Ibid.,* xii, § 4. Cf. Gottlob Frege, *The Foundations of Arithmetic,* trans. J.L. Austin (2d rev. ed.; New York: Harper & Bros., 1960 [Harper Torchbooks]), p. 2: "The aim of proof is . . . not merely to place the truth of a proposition beyond all doubt, but also to afford us insight into the dependence of truths upon one another. . . . The further we pursue these enquiries [into the foundations of mathematics], the fewer become the primitive truths to which we reduce everything; and this simplification is in itself a goal worth pursuing."
69. *N. E.,* IV, vii, § 19.
70. *N. E.,* I, i, § 19.
71. Leibniz, of course, believes that the principle of identity is innate: cf. *N. E.,* Bk. I.
72. Cf. Bertrand Russell, *Introduction to Mathematical Philosophy* (London: George Allen and Unwin, 1919), p. 2: "The most obvious and easy things in mathematics are not those that come logically at the

beginning; they are things that, from the point of view of logical deduction, come somewhere in the middle."

73. Cf. Frege, *op. cit.*, p. 3: "In general . . . the question of how we arrive at the content of a judgment should be kept distinct from the other question, Whence do we derive the justification for its assertion?"

74. *N. E.*, IV, xii, § 4. Cf. *O. F.*, p. 539: "we achieve the most perfect understanding [of truths] when without trusting to imagination or sense we reduce everything to notions."

75. *N. E.*, IV, xii, 4.

76. *Ibid.*

77. *N. E.*, IV, xii, §§ 4-6. Cf. Frege, *op. cit.*, p. 1: "a mere moral conviction" is "not good enough" in mathematics. We have noted above that Descartes himself admits in the *Principia* that propositions once thought "self-evidently" true have come to be regarded as false.

78. See Donnellan, *op. cit.*, pp. 67-68.

79. *Essay*, IV, viii, §§ 2-3.

80. *Ibid.*, § 6; cf § 4.

81. *Ibid.*, § 8.

82. *Ibid.*

83. On the other hand, Locke would evidently treat some common non-identical maxims as trifling on the ground that they should properly be regarded as definitional: "As to other less general maxims [than the principles of identity and non-contradiction] many of them are no more than bare verbal propositions, and teach us nothing but the respect and import of names one to another. 'The whole is equal to all its parts': what real truth . . . does it teach us? What more is contained in that maxim, than what the signification of the word *totum*, or the *whole*, does of itself import?" (*Ibid.*, vii, § 11.) Cf. Hobbes' "proof" of this "maxim" from definitions.

84. (2d ed.; London: George Allen & Unwin, 1937), pp. 16-17. Russell seems to be implying in this passage either that "analytic proposition" is a nonsensical expression or that there are non-tautologous analytic truths.

85. *Locke's Theory of Knowledge and its Historical Relations* (Cambridge: Cambridge University Press, 1960), p. 295. Cf. Frege's comment on the Leibnizian view that all the laws of number are analytic, *op. cit.*, p. 22: "But this view, too, has its difficulties. Can the great tree of the science of number as we know it, towering, spreading, and still continually growing, have its roots in bare identities? And how do the empty forms of logic come to disgorge so rich a content?"
86. *Essay*, VI, viii, § 3.
87. *N. E.*, IV, viii, § 3.
88. The date of the first ed. of *The Philosophy of Leibniz*.
89. *Introduction to Mathematical Philosophy* (London: George Allen & Unwin, 1919), p. 204.
90. *Ibid.*, p. 145.
91. *Ibid.*, p. 203. Russell admits that he cannot define "tautology" (cf. Morton White, *Toward Reunion in Philosophy* [Cambridge: Harvard University Press, 1956], pp. 130-132.)
92. I.M. Bochenski, *A History of Formal Logic*, trans. and ed. Ivo Thomas (Notre Dame: University of Notre Dame Press, 1961), p. 258.

CHAPTER III

SOME CRITICAL CHALLENGES TO LEIBNIZ' DOCTRINE OF NECESSITY

In this chapter Leibniz' definition of necessity will be examined and evaluated with reference to certain objections or questions suggested not so much by philosophical controversies of Leibniz' own time as by more recent critical discussion of problems relating directly or indirectly to the problem of necessity. Two general types of objection will be considered. In the first section I shall deal with the challenge--inspired in part by G.E. Moore's use of the "open question" argument--that Leibniz' proposed definition of a necessary truth as one reducible to the principle of non-contradiction cannot represent an adequate and self-sufficient analysis of the concept of necessity, since it seems entirely intelligible to inquire, "But is the principle of non-contradiction *necessary*?"[1] It will be found that Leibniz does regard this as an intelligible question which admits of an affirmative answer. What implications this fact has for his general doctrine will, of course, require investigation. In the second section we shall assess Leibniz' ability to reply to objections that several specific classes of truths which he certainly regarded as necessary are not, in fact, susceptible to reduction to the principle of identity by the substitution of definitions.

1. THE "NECESSITY" OF THE PRINCIPLE OF NON-CONTRADICTION

We have noted in chapter 1 that Leibniz treats "of the form of, or reducible to the principle of non-contradiction (identity)" as *the definition* of "necessarily true." The Moorean critic we have already conjured up is dissatisfied with this definition. He points out that "expressly or implicitly identical" can not *mean* "necessary," since it makes perfect sense to inquire, "but is the principle of identity *necessary*?" This question points up the fact that Leibniz' definition does not seem to take account of the connotations of inevitability or indispensability which have traditionally adhered to this term. To say that a proposition is (expressly or implicitly) identical does not seem to be at all the same as to say that it *has to be true*.

Leibniz' view of the necessity of the principle.--There can be no question that Leibniz himself admits--at least implicitly--that the question of the necessity of the principle itself *is* an intelligible one. Consider the following statements:

(1) Whatever implies a contradiction is impossible, for this is to say nothing.[2]

(2) Thus the principle of contradiction is the principle of all truths of reason, and if it is given up [sublato] all reasoning is given up [tollitur]. . . .[3]

(3) [The principle of contradiction is] the foundation of all Logic; and if it disappears [cesse] there is no way of reasoning with certitude.[4]

(4) I was surprised to see . . . that he denies in divine matters this great principle which says: that things which are the same as a third thing are themselves the same [sont les même entre elles]. This is to give the victory to the adversaries without realizing it and to take away all certainty from all reasoning [oster toute certitude à tout raisonnement]. . . . But how can faith decree anything, which overthrows a principle without which all belief and affirmation or negation would be vain [sans lequel toute creance et affirmation ou negation seroit

vaine]? *It must therefore necessarily be the case [il faut donc necessairement] that two propositions which are true at the same time are not complete contradictories [ne soyent pointe tout à fait contradictoires] ....*[5]

Passages (1) and (4) indicate that Leibniz did not, in the last analysis, wish to hold that "reducible to identity" is the full *meaning* of "necessary," nor "reducible to contradiction," of "impossible." For both passages suggest that one can give a reason *why* what is reducible to identity or contradiction *is* (respectively) necessary or impossible: "whatever implies a contradiction is impossible, *for* this is to say nothing"; "it must *therefore necessarily* be the case [that two true propositions are not contradictories]". But if "being necessary" *meant* "being reducible to identity" (or "impossible," " ... contradiction"), it would be as absurd to look for reasons why the identical is necessary or the contradictory impossible as to look for reasons why bachelors are unmarried. The four passages taken together make it clear that when Leibniz says that the principle of non-contradiction is necessary he means that it is in some sense an indispensable condition of reasoning or knowledge itself. This point is explicit in (2) and (3), and at least implicit in (4). His position closely parallels that of Aristotle: if there is to be meaningful discourse (reasoning), the affirmation of any statement must be taken to exclude the denial. As Leibniz elsewhere expresses it, the principle of non-contradiction is "in some sense ... involved in the definitions of the true and the false."[6]

There are two points to be noted in connection with this use of "necessary" in application to the principle of non-contradiction itself. In the first place, it is not clear that "necessary" in this use is susceptible of definition in non-modal terms. To say the necessary is the indispensable is not to offer such a definition, since "indispensable" can only be explained as "that which *cannot* be dispensed with." It seems that we must concede this point to the Moorean critic. Secondly, the necessity involved appears to be only a relative necessity: the principle is necessary *if there is to be* significant discourse. This might suggest the danger of an infinite regress, since it invites the questions of whether "significant discourse" is necessary.

Leibniz seems, indeed, to invite the latter challenge in one passage in the *Nouveaux Essais*. The subject under discussion is possible types of argument and Leibniz proposes as an addition to Locke's list (*ad ignorantiam, ad hominem*, etc.) the argument *ad vertiginem*,[7] as when one argues thus:

> If this proof is not accepted, we have no way of arriving at certainty on the point in question, which is taken as an absurdity.[8]

Leibniz adds that this argument is good "en certain cas,"

> as in a case where someone wished to deny the immediate and primitive truths, for example, that nothing can be and not be at the same time . . . , because if he was right we would have no way of knowing anything. But when one has propounded certain principles and wishes to maintain them because otherwise the whole system of some received doctrine would fall; the argument is not decisive: Because one must distinguish between what is necessary to support our knowledge [pour soutenir nos connoissances], and what serves as the foundation of our received doctrines or our practices.[9]

Unfortunately, he does not provide any direct elaboration of the evidently crucial distinction presented in the last sentence of this passage. Instead he goes on to discuss two cases in which the argument has been *in*appropriately employed. In criticizing the second of these--an attempt to justify debasing the coinage on the grounds that without doing so one "could not coin money without losing it"--he remarks that this argument assumes "that a practice is necessary which is in fact not. Because there is neither order from heaven nor human law which obliges people to coin money who have neither a mine nor the opportunity to possess silver bars."[10] Although the point is nowhere clearly spelled out, this passage seems to leave us with the suggestion that reasoning or having knowledge is entirely necessary, whereas many (or most? or all?) other practices, not to mention the upholding of "received doctrines" of various sorts, are not. But it is very hard to see how such a contention could be supported. Certainly not by reference to "divine command or human law." And in any case, of *whatever* might be brought forward to justify the "necessity" of reasoning, it could presumably be asked whether *it* was itself necessary.

There is however, another way of understanding the contention that the principle of non-contradiction is necessary because it is an indispensable condition of knowledge which does not seem to me to invite the charge of setting up an infinite regress, and which seems also to represent more accurately Leibniz' real thought on the subject. We may say that the principle of non-contradiction is necessary, not because it is the necessary condition of one practice among others, which practice is itself necessary, etc.; but because, as the necessary condition of meaningful affirmation and denial, it cannot itself be meaningfully denied.[11] (Or, a distinction between truth and falsity being, on Leibniz's view, possible only as long as the principle of non-contradiction is accepted, it cannot make sense to assert that the principle is false. In this respect it differs radically from all other propositions, however necessary their acceptance may be for certain special systems or practices, and however "necessary" the acceptance of these systems or practices may seem in some respect or other.) The point is *not* that we must accept the principle of non-contradiction in order to reason, *and we must reason*; but rather that a principle which is the necessary condition of reasoning itself cannot intelligibly be challenged, since any challenge of the truth of a principle must take place *within the framework* of rational discourse. The principle is therefore an *absolutely necessary truth* (in the new, indefinable sense of "necessary"), providing we accept the Aristotelian-Leibnizian point that it *is* an indispensable condition of logic and reasoning.

Implications for the doctrine of necessary truth.--We must now take up the question of how Leibniz' willingness to argue for the "necessity" of the principle of non-contradiction bears on his thesis that "necessary" is to be defined as "of the form of, or reducible to, an express identity." The important alternative possibilities that need to be considered are the following:

(1) There are two mutually independent senses of "necessary" involved here, and is it strictly accidental that the principle Leibniz takes as *defining* "necessary" in one sense turns out to be itself necessary in the other sense.

(2) (Almost the opposite of (1)) No purely formal criterion, such as reducibility to some form of the principle of non-contradiction, can provide a satisfactory definition of "necessity," since connotations of inevitability, indispensability, etc. are essential to the meaning of this term, and no principle or schema can establish its own inevitability. (It is thus that we do intuitively regard the question, "but is the principle of non-contradiction *necessary*; is it necessary that A be A, that 'A is not-A' be regarded as false, etc.? as an *open* question.) It is nonsense to speak of an independent sense of "necessary" which has no such connotations. The definition in terms of non-contradiction could amount to no more than an empty and arbitrary manipulation of signs which is simply irrelevant as a reply to substantive questions about necessity, unless it can be shown that this principle and its instances, and these propositions alone, are inevitable in some epistemologically ultimate sense. On this view, then, the principle of non-contradiction owes its acceptability as a significant criterion of necessity wholly to the fact that it is a necessary and sufficient criterion of what might be called "epistemological indispensability."

(3) (Compromise position) The plausibility and relevance of the identity criterion of necessity (or the general proposal of "identical" as the definition of "necessary") is neither entirely independent of the special epistemological status of this principle nor entirely a function of this status. It might be held, for instance, that a "necessary truth" in the important traditional sense of "logical necessity" can best be characterized as one which *both* partakes of some sort of indispensability or inevitability *and* has certain specific formal properties or satisfies a formal criterion. Considered in connection with Leibniz' position, this view would allow one to admit that the implicit acceptance of some propositions besides the principle of non-contradiction might be viewed as a necessary condition of meaningful discourse, without entailing the relinquishment of the principle as *the* criterion of logical necessity; and at the same time to hold that considerations of the principle's "epistemological indispensability" are not simply irrelevant to its use in the definition of logical necessity.

In the absence of explicit discussion in his own writings, we cannot know with certainty which of these alternatives Leibniz would have preferred, nor indeed whether he would have rejected all of them in favor of some approach not considered here. However, there are some points that can be drawn from his work, which, together with certain general philosophical considerations, do seem to throw light on this rather important question.

(1) The suggestion that Leibniz' conception of logical necessity was purely formal, and that he therefore would have been prepared to treat questions of the "certainty" or "indispensability" of the principle itself as irrelevant to its use in the definition of necessity, is rendered extremely implausible by the fact that Leibniz never makes a sharp distinction between the "necessity" and the "certainty" of an axiom, mathematical proposition, or other necessary truth. As we have already seen, the notion of establishing the necessity of a proposition by reducing it to identity is bound up, in his thought, with the geometrical ideal of providing formal proofs wherever possible--even of "obvious" truths. To reduce a proposition to identity is not, for Leibniz, merely to show the "necessity" of the proposition in a bare formal sense of the term, but to *prove* it--to establish its "infallible and perpetual certainty."[12] This point is made over and over in the *Nouveaux Essais* and elsewhere in his writings. It is true that Leibniz occasionally speaks of the principle of non-contradiction as an "assumption."[13] This might imply either that he, even more than Aristotle, was not always altogether satisfied that the arguments he could put behind the "indispensability" of this principle were overwhelmingly successful, or that at certain times he felt inclined to admit a distinction between a principle's being "indispensable to rational discourse and its being "certainly true". By far the more dominant line of thought, however, is represented by his insistence on the point that reduction to identity, and this alone, can establish the universality and certainty, *in* establishing the necessity, of any true proposition.[14] To show that a proposition is reducible to identity is not, for Leibniz, merely to show that it is "necessary" in some attenuated formal sense, only remotely related to the traditional understanding of the term: it is still, for him, to demonstrate as well that what the proposition asserts "must be the case."[15]

(2) On the other hand, the suggestion that reducibility to identity is relevant to the problem of necessity *only* in so far as it provides the adequate criterion of "epistemological indispensability" does not seem to be a possible alternative for Leibniz. In the first place, acceptance of this alternative would apparently force us to regard as rather pointless his persistent emphasis on identity or non-contradiction as providing *the definition* of necessity. It must be noted in this connection that remarks about the indispensability of the principle of identity are seldom found in the context of his discussions of logical necessity *per se*. They rather tend to occur when he is considering the principle as a "first principle" or a "primitive and immediate truth." And this brings us to what seems to me the decisive point. There are, in Leibniz' view, primitive contingent truths or "truths of fact" ("I exist," "I perceive different things [varia a me percipiantur]"), as well as primitive truths of reason (the principle of identity and such "express" instances of it as a "a rectangle is a rectangle").[16] The former, though contingent, share epistemological indispensability with the primitive truths of reason or identities.[17] For instance, in one place Leibniz writes:

> These two first principles: Identities are true, and propositions implying a contradiction are false, the other of experience [sic]: that different things [varia] are perceived by me, are such, that from them it is possible to demonstrate, first, that demonstration of them is impossible; secondly that all other propositions depend on [pendere] them, or [sive] if these two principles are not true, there is no truth and knowledge whatsoever [nullam omnino veritatem et cognitionem locum habere]. Therefore either they are admitted without difficulty or all search for truth is given up.[18]

There are, of course, a number of serious problems which arise in connection with passages such as this. For one thing, while Leibniz here suggests that all truths of fact depend on the "varia a me percipiantur," he elsewhere makes it clear that he regards "I exist" as *another* primitive truth of fact.[19] Secondly, in a great many well-known passages, Leibniz indicates that, as truths of reason depend on the Principle of Identity, truths of fact depend upon the

Principle of Sufficient Reason.[20] And it is of the *latter* principle (and not "I exist," or "I perceive different things"), together with the principle of identity, that he says: "it may be said in some sense that these two principles are involved in the definition of the True and the False."[21] Moreover, this still leaves untouched the important *further* question of how, precisely, all truths of fact may be said to "depend" on the primitive truths. However, such obscurities and apparent contradictions in Leibniz' assertions about the "first truths of fact" are immaterial in the present context. The important point to observe is merely that, while Leibniz regards the principle of identity as "epistemologically indispensable," he evidently does *not* regard epistemological indispensability as *constituting* logical necessity, since it may, on his express view, be present where logical necessity is absent--namely, in the "first truth(s) of fact."

(3) We are thus brought to consider the third alternative, which now seems the most workable interpretation of the three. On this view the identity criterion has a double aspect. On the one hand, Leibniz uses it to preserve and give definite formal significance to the traditional notion that a necessary truth is one of which the opposite is "self-contradictory." In doing so, however, he apparently runs the risk of turning necessity into a strictly formal concept, sheared of all connotations of inevitability or indispensability. These connotations are reintroduced, however, by taking account of (or assuming) the epistemological indispensability of the identity principle itself. But to deny an instance of this principle entails denial of the principle. Thus all logically necessary truths will be on Leibniz' view in a sense entailed by the very possibility of knowledge and truth.[22] Like suggestion (1), this alternative admits a logical distinction between "necessity" understood as indubitability, and "necessity" as "contradictoriness of the opposite." It denies, however, that considerations of indubitability or indispensability of the principle of non-contradiction are irrelevant to the effort to account for or define necessity in terms of this principle.

Ontological inevitability.--It must further be noted, however, that Leibniz in many places indicates that he does not regard the principle of non-contradiction as *merely* a necessary condition of rational discourse. It may also be construed as an ontological principle, which has some implications for the structure of all possible worlds. In its ontological employment the principle is formulated in terms of being: it is in some sense ontologically inevitable that "rien ne peut estre et n'estre pas en même temps."[23] He indicates sometimes, particularly in later works, that the contingent laws of nature which obtain in this actual world are in some sense under the governance of the eternal or necessary truths (which are, of course, ultimately based on the principle of non-contradiction). In such contexts he speaks of necessary truths as "existing" independently of all human intelligence, having their ground in the eternal intelligence of God.[24] In *De rerum originatione radicali*, for instance, he writes: "temporal, contingent, or physical truths arise out of eternal truths which are essential or metaphysical."[25] And again "we observe that everything in the world happens in accordance with the laws of the eternal truths."[26] Thus it is often said that for Leibniz the world is "rational" or "logical" throughout.[27]

As no useful critical discussion of any single aspect of Leibniz' metaphysical system is possible without reference to every other aspect, and as such a full discussion of his system would take us very far from our immediate subject, I do not propose here to enter into any more detailed examination of his conception of ontological necessity, nor of the ontological status of the principle of non-contradiction. We shall, however, touch again on the metaphysical correlates or underpinnings of Leibniz' doctrine of necessary truth when we come to examine his arguments against conventionalism.

The unique status of the principle of non-contradiction.--It may reasonably be enquired at this point whether Leibniz really has adequate grounds for attributing to the principle of non-contradiction the unique status of *the* first truth of reason. The arguments, if they may be called that, which he advances in support of this position appear to be two. First is the contention, already alluded to, that the principle is "in some sense involved in the definition of the true and the false." By this he seems to mean that the notions of truth and falsity involve the notions of affirmation and denial, while these in turn cannot be understood without reference to the principle that the negation of a true proposition is false, and the negation of a false proposition is true. Secondly, he writes that "identical propositions are the primary propositions of all, and so true *per se*, for certainly nothing can be found which like a middle term connects something with itself. . . . "[28] The first point indicates that "it would not make sense to doubt" the principle of identity. The second presents, as it were, an elaboration of the assertion that identities are not subject to demonstration by "reduction" to "more basic" propositions. However, if such considerations establish anything, they appear to establish only that the principle of identity is *a* "first truth of reason." They do not seem in any way to preclude the possibility that other reasons could be advanced for regarding other principles as "first truths of reason."

Indeed, the *main* reason behind Leibniz' insistence on the uniqueness of the principle of non-contradiction (identity) appears to be simply his belief that all other "truths of reason" (including, pre-eminently, the propositions of mathematics and logic) can in fact be reduced to it. The critical issue for his doctrine of necessity is therefore the extent to which this belief may be justified. This question we shall now consider.

2. DIRECT CHALLENGES TO THE VIEW THAT ALL NECESSARY TRUTHS ARE REDUCIBLE TO FORMAL IDENTITIES

Negative necessary truths.--There is one rather obvious difficulty suggested by the assertion that all necessary truths are express or implicit identities which we may deal with first. If an "identity" is a proposition expressly or implicitly of the form, "A is A," or "AB is A," or "All A is A," and all necessary truths are identities, the implication would appear to be that all necessary truths are affirmative. Certainly, if "All bodies are extended" is a necessary truth, "No bodies are unextended" would appear equally to be one. But the latter proposition reduces to "No A is not-A," not to "All A is A." And in "No A is not-A," the "relation between subject and predicate" is clearly not one of identity.[29]

There is, moreover, an analogous difficulty for the definition of "impossible." The evidently "impossible" assertion, "No bodies are extended," reduces not to "A is not-A," but to "Not (A is A)," where the relation between subject and predicate is clearly not one of contradiction. If no way can be found around these difficulties, Leibniz' doctrine would surely have to be dismissed as too strongly counterintuitive to be of any possible use in illuminating the concept of necessary truth.

I think it must be allowed that Leibniz' philosophy is in general characterized by an excessive preoccupation with the affirmative form of propositions. For instance, as Couturat has shown, Leibniz' efforts to develop logical calculi are crippled by a failure to cope adequately with negative propositions--a failure which may perhaps in turn be traced to his "marked predilection" for the "intensional" rather than the "extensional" point of view in dealing with the systematization of logic.[30] As Couturat remarks, Leibniz "repeats endlessly, as if by habit, that the predicate is contained in the subject."[31] Leibniz often, indeed, cites the "containment" of the predicate in the subject as the criterion or definition of truth--sometimes adding and sometimes neglecting to add that this holds exclusively for *affirmative* propositions.[32]

Leibniz does, however, recognize the existence of negative necessary truths, and he attempts to fit them into his "identity" theory of necessity by introducing, in the *Nouveaux Essais*, the somewhat paradoxical expression "negative identities" ("identiques negatives").[33] Examples of negative identities are the following: "What is A cannot be not-A"; "An equilateral rectangle cannot be a non-rectangle"; "It is true that every man is an animal, therefore it is false that there is a man who is not an animal." These, he says, are true by the principle of non-contradiction ("sont du principe de contradiction"). He adds:

> The principle of contradiction is in general: a proposition is either true or false; which includes two statements; the first, that the true and the false are not compatible in the same proposition, or that a proposition cannot be true and false at the same time. The other, that the opposite or the negation of the true and the false are not compatible, or that there is no

middle term between the true and the false, or further, that there can be no proposition which is neither true nor false.[34]

It must be remembered, however, that Leibniz thinks of the principles of identity and non-contradiction as being fundamentally the *same* principle. (That he also regards the law of excluded middle as part of the principle of non-contradiction is evident from the passage just quoted.) The conclusion to be drawn from all this is therefore, I believe, that Leibniz is prepared to regard all propositions *true* by virtue of the principle of identity-or-contradiction as "identities," whether or not the predicate follows by identity from the subject, and all propositions *false* by virtue of this principle as "contradictories," whether or not the predicate term is in fact the negation of the subject or part of the subject. In spite of the fact that Leibniz' way of speaking and the examples he uses often suggest the contrary, the identity-contradiction criterion of necessity[35] has to do with the overall form of the proposition, rather than specifically with the relation between subject and predicate terms. "Not (A is not-A)" or "No A is not-A" must thus be counted among the "express identities"; "Not (A is A)" or "No A is A" among the "contradictories." He further adds: "one may vary these statements [included under the general designation, "principle of non-contradiction"] in many ways and apply them to hypotheticals, copulatives, disjunctives, and others."[36]

It therefore appears that Leibniz' "identity criterion" is not, in fact, so restrictive as to exclude negative truths, and that these do not constitute a real difficulty for this doctrine. The next class of truths to be considered are not, however, so easily accommodated.

"Disparates," "necessary coexistents," and "incompatibles."--The propositions to be considered here are those which assert the *difference* of two "ideas," e.g., "white is not red," "yellowness is not sweetness," etc.; and those which asserts that one attribute either *excludes* another (e.g., "what is white is not black") or necessarily coexists with another (e.g., "what is colored is extended"). Although the "disparates" must be distinguished from the "incompatibles" (mere difference does not entail incompatibility: although yellowness is not sweetness, what is yellow "all over" may at the same time be sweet "all over"), propositions of the two groups present the same problem

for Leibniz' theory of necessity: they seem to be necessary (certainly not "contingent"), and they appear at the same time to be completely irreducible to *any* general axiom, including, of course, the principle of identity. It is certainly *nonsense* to assert that "yellowness is sweetness," or that "object o is completely red and completely white," but can such assertions be said to involve *contradictions*? They are clearly not in any sense formally self-contradictory propositions.

The difficulties which these propositions create for any "analytic" doctrine of necessary truth have been much emphasized and extensively discussed in the philosophical literature of recent years.[37] It is therefore perhaps the most disappointing feature of Leibniz' development of his doctrine that he takes up these truths for discussion in the *Nouveaux Essais*, only to brush them aside with vague and even meaningless remarks. Moreover, his thought, in so far as it is possible to follow it, seems to be studded with inconsistencies.

The disparates he deals with in Book I and again in Book IV. In the earlier passage he does not give any indication of questioning the view that they are necessary; in the later one he expressly classifies them as necessary truths. In Book I he begins by asserting that these propositions are "identities or almost identities" ("[elles] sont identiques, ou peut s'en faut"), and adds that "the identities or immediates do not receive proof" ("les identiqiues ou immediates ne reçoivent point de preuve").[38] He does not, however, explain how a proposition can be "almost an identity," but merely offers the highly puzzling "clarification" that these truths involve the application of the "general maxim to particular cases."[39] A few lines later he argues against Locke that the principle of contradiction is more basic than Locke's maxim, "the same thing is not different":

> For it appears to me that one allows himself more freedom in advancing that A is not B than in saying that A is not not-A. And the reason which prevents A from being B is that B involves not-A [Et la raison qui empeche A d'etre B, est que B enveloppe non A].[40]

This is certainly consistent with his general doctrine of necessity, but appears precisely to commit him to being able to show by analysis that, e.g., "yellowness" involves or contains "not-sweetness"--that "yellowness is not sweetness" can be formally reduced to "yellowness is not not-yellowness." One could hardly imagine a more explicit indication that such a reduction is possible. In the following section, moreover, he actually says, in reply to Locke's contention that truths such as "a square is not a circle," "red is not green," are known immediately, that these propositions are in fact known as conclusions from the general maxims, although the maxims may be employed only implicitly.[41] But aside from being intrinsically implausible, this position appears flatly to contradict his previous assertion that such truths are immediate, being "almost identities," and hence "receive no proof." And Leibniz gives no explanation whatsoever of how the disparates may be seen or shown to follow from the principle of non-contradiction.

The issue is rendered, if possible, still more obscure by the fact that in Book IV Leibniz classes the disparates as "negative identities," and says that they are primitive, but explicitly contrasts them with the primitive truths which are "contradictories."

> I come now to the negative identities which are either true by
> the principle of contradiction, or are disparates [qui sont ou du
> principe de contradiction, ou des disparates].[42]

He gives some standard examples of primitive truths which are true by virtue of the principle of contradiction: "what is A cannot be not-A," "AB cannot be not-A," etc. He then proceeds:

> As for the Disparates these are those propositions which say,
> that the object of one idea is not the object of another idea;
> e.g., that heat is not the same thing as color, or man and animal
> are not the same, although every man may be an animal.[43]

These, he says, "can be assured independently of any proof or of the reduction to opposition or to the principle of contradiction, when these ideas are well enough understood so as not to here have need of analysis...."[44] Although Leibniz does not here explicitly concede that the disparates *cannot* be reduced to identity, but says only that they do not *need* proof, he clearly implies that they are *not* instances of the principle of contradiction by contrasting them with truths that *are* instances, and by characterizing them as primitives. He seems, therefore, to have abandoned completely the view expressed in Book I, that what "prevents" A from being B in such cases is that B involves not-A. He does not explain his classification of them as "negative identities," but this classification may perhaps be understood with reference to the fact that such truths do involve a *denial of identity*. They lack, however, the formal property which Leibniz emphasizes everywhere else as being the distinguishing feature of primitives. That Leibniz was constrained, in order to accommodate these truths, to set aside his formal criterion of necessity, must perhaps be regarded as constituting a virtual refutation of his doctrine. These truths are necessary, *but* their denial is not formally self-contradictory nor reducible to a formal self-contradiction: therefore "necessity" cannot be defined as that of which the opposite implies a formal self-contradiction.

As the last quotation suggests, however, Leibniz is not inclined to treat all disparates as primitives, but only those in which the ideas are "assés entendues pour n'avoir point besoin ici d'analyse." Otherwise, he says, "one can make a mistake, for in saying, the triangle and the trilateral are not the same, one errs, since ... the three sides and the three angles always go together." He adds that one can, in any case, always say in the abstract that triangularity is not trilaterality; or that the "formal reason of triangle and trilateral are not the same, as the Philosophers say. They are different aspects [raports] of the same thing."[45] But what these remarks seem to add up to is not so much the point that some disparates are non-primitive (whether or not this is the case it is not necessary to decide here), but rather that one must distinguish *between the assertion that two ideas or attributes are different*, and the *denial that two attributes always go together*, or that there is some necessary connection between two ideas. Real disparates, he seems to believe, are always true ("on peut toujours dire dans l'abstrait ... "); but corresponding denials of necessary coexistence are not always true--one has to be cautious in respect to *them*. Confusion arises because the same sentence can be interpreted either as a disparate or a denial of necessary coexistence:

thus, "the triangle is not the trilateral," could be read either as the true statement that the "idea" of triangularity is different from the idea of trilaterality (disparate), or the false statement that there *can be* a triangle which is not a trilateral.[46]

Leibniz himself seems to have felt these distinctions rather than seen them. He does not otherwise discuss the relation or distinction between disparates and denials of necessary coexistence. He does, however, deal briefly with the question of necessary exclusion and necessary coexistence in another passage in the *Nouveaux Essais*. And this passage tends to confirm the point that Leibniz' definition of "necessity" is not adequate to accommodate all the truths which he is prepared to regard as necessary.

At IV, vi, § 10 Leibniz quotes Locke's suggestion that we cannot be certain of any "necessary coexistence or incompatibility" of secondary qualities, besides those "which belong to the same sense, and necessarily exclude each other, as when [Leibniz continues in his own words] one says that what is black is not white [ce que est blanc n'est pas noir]."[47] Leibniz' reply is interesting in two respects. In the first place, he makes no comment on the example he puts into Philalethis' mouth ("what is white is not black"), thereby implicitly agreeing with the view that it is a necessary truth. Moreover, he contests the point that relations between secondary qualities of different senses are never necessary:

> I think, however, that some could perhaps be found; for example, every palpable body . . . is visible. Every hard body makes a noise, when it is struck in air.[48]

Does Leibniz wish to hold that these propositions are identities? That they are provable by the principle of non-contradiction? Since he gives no indication, one can only conclude that he would be defenseless against contentions that these represent "synthetic" necessary truths--involving, perhaps, some "intuition" of necessary connection or exclusion. But if Leibniz' definition of "necessity" in terms of "formal reducibility to identity" were accepted, the expression "synthetic necessary truth" would be nonsensical. Leibniz is not in a position to hold that it is nonsensical, since his own writings apparently commit him to the view that there *are* such truths. Therefore Leibniz' own statements seem to force us to conclude that the definition is not satisfactory, and that his doctrine must be rejected.

It might be held, however, that even if reducibility to identity cannot provide an adequate definition of necessity, it might still be construed as *an important criterion* of necessity; and in particular, that the principle of non-contradiction (identity) is in some sense the ground of the necessity of logical and mathematical truths. We must now therefore inquire whether Leibniz is in a position to uphold at least this more limited thesis. We shall find that he is, in fact, quite far from being able to do so.

Mathematical and logical truths.--Leibniz' treatment of the propositions of mathematics and logic is somewhat less unsatisfactory than his treatment of disparates, incompatibles, and assertions of necessary coexistence, in that he does make some direct and serious efforts to show how a number of such truths may be derived from identities by means of definitions. His efforts along these lines are, however, far less extensive and far more fragmentary than one might be led to expect from the frequency and firmness with which he asserts that the principle of identity is the sole basis of all truths of reason. Kauppi's statement that Leibniz "illustrates" his general thesis by offering some reductions[49] is precise: and there is certainly a world of difference between "illustrating" a thesis and establishing it. Aside from proofs already mentioned of "a whole is greater than its part" and "two and two are four," propositions of which Leibniz offers demonstrations include the principle of the syllogism,[50] the Euclidean axiom equals added to equals yield equals,"[51] the proposition that space has three dimensions,[52] and various logical principles such as the symmetry and transitivity of identity.[53] Interesting as these and other proofs constructed by Leibniz may be, they are not nearly extensive and systematic enough to constitute a general demonstration of the derivability of all mathematics and logic from the principle of identity. As we have already seen that his *general* reasons for holding this principle to be the one primitive truth of reason are vague and uncompelling, the conclusion is unavoidable that the exclusive primacy of the principle of identity-non-contradiction has somewhat the status, in Leibniz' system, of an article of faith. (It is significant, in this connection, that in his very early work, the *Dissertation de arte combinatoria*, the principle of non-contradiction is already announced as "the primary truth of all theorems or necessary propositions":[54] the general thesis is adopted from tradition at the outset; "illustrations" are gradually worked out in the course of Leibniz' career.) Pap's remark that the reducibility of all necessary truths to identities "was by no means merely a dogmatic claim of Leibniz' "[55] thus requires qualification. It is true that Leibniz went beyond the Aristotelians and Scholastics in attempting to give real *significance* to the ancient doctrine of the primacy of the principle of non-contradiction; it is not true that he provided sufficient *evidence* to remove the doctrine from the realm of dogma to the realm of established theory.[56]

This point would, I believe, hold even if the demonstrations which Leibniz presents were all rigorous and successful. But, as is now well-known, there is a further difficulty. A number of the derivations which Leibniz does present are not effective testimony to the primacy of the principle of identity because they are not perfectly rigorous. For instance, as Frege has pointed out, Leibniz tacitly assumes the law of association in his proof of "2+2=4," although the only axiom stated for this proof is the principle of identity.[57]

As far as I have been able to discover, Leibniz nowhere in his published writings states *this* principle in connection with any of his demonstrations. On the other hand, it is important to realize that in his sketches for the development of logical calculi, Leibniz does very frequently explicitly admit as primitive axioms other basic principles of modern logic such as the law of permutation (or commutation) and the law of tautology.[58] Sometimes these are given a different status from those principles which he regards as true by the principle of non-contradiction. Thus, in one "specimen" Leibniz lists the following principles as axioms or "propositiones per se verae":

    a est a
    ab est a
    a non est non-a
    non-a non est a
    que non est a, est non-a

qui non est non-a, est a.[59]

He lists as a "consequentia per se vera" the principle of the syllogism, and then gives a list of five "principles of the calculus," which include the law of tautology and the law of permutation. He does not speak of reducing these to identity. In another sketch he lists these principles, together with the principle of identity (A is A) as "primary foundations of the logical calculus."[60] (Also included are A not = B non-A, and some principles which Leibniz would probably regard as definitions: e.g., A= not not-A, which he elsewhere[61] explicitly characterizes as "the definition or the use of the sign *not*.") In yet another sketch these two principles (permutation and tautology) are stated as the two axioms of the calculus.[62]

In efforts at working out his calculi, therefore, Leibniz finds himself admitting axioms or primitive principles other than the principle of non-contradiction. But the development of a logical calculus was always identified in his mind with the project of making possible the demonstration of truths of reason.[63] On the other hand, the demonstration of truths of reason was generally identified (as we have seen) with the enterprise of establishing their necessity.[64] It can only be pointed out that demonstration within calculi such as Leibniz sketches, with their various non-identical primitive principles, would not establish necessity as Leibniz defines it.

On this account, the implicit assumption of the associative law in the proof of "2+2=4" may be treated as just one aspect of a more general shortcoming in the support which Leibniz is able to offer for his doctrine. The issue is clouded by the fact that he apparently never recognizes the need for *this particular* principle in developing the calculi that are to be the instruments of his proofs. Aside from that, however, there seems to be no reason why he should have been any less ready to admit the law of association than the permutative law, which does appear in the calculi. The *first* question, therefore, is how Leibniz could reconcile his *actual admission* in his logic of primitive principles besides the principle of identity with the doctrine that there are no primitive truths of reason besides this law. If the answer is that they are admitted only provisionally, until a method of eliminating them is devised,[65] we must reply that in that case the exclusive primacy of the principle of identity-non-contradiction can rightfully only be treated as an *hypothesis*. Leibniz however, consistently presents it not as an hypothesis but as a fact.

One may at this point raise the question of how much of Leibniz' general doctrine of necessity survives in the work of more recent philosophers who support the enterprise of reducing mathematics and logic to as few primitive logical truths as possible, but deny that one can get along with the principle of identity as the only axiom or primitive principle. To this I think it must be replied that very little survives. The interest of Leibniz' theory lay in the attempted connection of the traditional intuitive notion of necessity (opposite impossible) with a precise formal criterion, via the concept of self-contradictoriness: impossible means self-contradictory and self-contradictory means expressly or implicitly of the form "A is not-A", "not (A is A)," etc. It was only because of this apparent connection that Leibniz was able to maintain so firmly the equivalence of reducing mathematical and logical truths to primitives and demonstrating the necessity of these truths. Modern works such as the *Principia Mathematica*, while they out-Leibniz Leibniz in endeavoring actually to carry out his cherished aim of reducing a vast body of truths to a very few simple notions, do so precisely at the expense of his theory of necessity, which, however original in many of its aspects, derived significance and relevance from its strong roots in traditional understanding and discussion of the concept. (It is no doubt significant that recent discussions of the status of mathematical and logical truths, in relation to the work of the logistic theorists, have tended to concentrate on the more recent and less traditional concept of analyticity, rather than the ancient question of necessity.)[66]

3. CONCLUSION

We have now seen that Leibniz' doctrine is unable to meet some of the most important challenges advanced by the twentieth century critic. More than that, however, we have discovered that the efforts which Leibniz makes to support his theory are limited and in some respects unimpressive. His treatment of the disparates, incompatibles, and assertions of necessary coexistence involve difficulties which are not subtle, but conspicuous. The thesis that all of mathematics and logic can be established through the employment of definitions and identical axioms alone is maintained with the most absolute conviction but relative meager substantiation. We have further noted that Leibniz himself is not consistent in treating "expressly or implicitly identical" as *the definition* of "necessary," since he is prepared to raise on another level the question of the necessity of the principle of identity (non-contradiction) itself.

Thus far, in evaluating Leibniz' theory, we have focused on the contention that the principle of identity is the first truth of reason, and the grounds of all necessary truth. Examination of this central tenet of the doctrine has been sufficient to reveal some serious limitations and deficiencies. I now propose to consider one other aspect of Leibniz' conception of the nature of necessary truth--the interest and importance of which is largely unaffected by doubts concerning the workability of the identity criterion. This is his view that although *definition* plays an essential role in the demonstration of propositions of logic, mathematics, etc., such propositions should not on that account be regarded as arbitrary, conventional, or "merely verbal."

NOTES

1. Cf. G.E. Moore, *Principia Ethica* (Cambridge: Cambridge University Press, 1959), pp. 15-16, 21. (The 1st ed. of this work appeared in 1903). White, *op. cit.*, pp. 127-132, criticizes recent discussion of analyticity from a similar point of view. The existence of this problem for Leibniz' definition has actually been indicated by Russell: "Necessity must mean something other than connection with the Law of Contradiction; the statement that analytic propositions are necessary is significant, and the opposite statement--that synthetic propositions are contingent--is certainly so regarded by Leibniz. It would seem that necessity is ultimate and indefinable." (*Philosophy of Leibniz*, p. 23).

2. From Leibniz' notes on Boyle's *Some Considerations about the Reconcileableness of Reason and Religion*, quoted (in translation) by Loemker in his article, "Boyle and Leibniz," *Journal of the History of Ideas*, XVI (1955), p. 38.

3. *G.*, IV, p. 237.

4. *T.*, p. 67.

5. *N.E.*, IV, xviii, § 1. The emphasis is in the text.

6. *T*, p. 419.

7. Called "*ad scepticismum*" in an earlier draft (cf. *N.E.*, p. 491.)

8. *N.E.*, IV, xvii, § 19.

9. *Ibid*. Note that the principle of non-contradiction is here expressed in the common Aristotelian form, in terms of "being."

10. *Ibid*.

11. Cf. (2), above: "Whatever implies a contradiction is impossible, for this is to say nothing."

12. *N.E.*, I, i, § 5. Cf. IV, vii, § 8: also *G.*, VI, pp. 503-504. Leibniz indicates in passages such as these that while sense experience of "induction" can suggest or confirm mathematics and other necessary truths, it cannot yield the knowledge of their certainty and universality which is to be achieved through reduction to first principles.

13. *G.*, VII, p. 299. (This passage begins: "I assume [assumo] first of all that every statement (i.e., affirmation or negation) is either true or false, and if the affirmation is true, the negation is false. . . . ") See also *G.*, II, p. 62.

14. Besides passages already cited in note 1, p. 118, see *N.E.*, IV, xii, §§ 1, 2, 4, 5, among many similar passages. Leibniz speaks of the principle of non-contradiction as "self-evident" much more often than he speaks of it as an "assumption." Thus, at *G.*, VII, p. 300 he says that identities are "true *per se.*" On the other hand it is not generally clear in such passages whether Leibniz is insisting on the positive point that identities are *true*, or merely emphasizing the negative point that they cannot be demonstrated: "Identical propositions are the first propositions of all, and insusceptible of any demonstration and so true *per se* [atque adeo per se verae]. . . . " (*Ibid.*)

15. Letter to Sophia Charlotte, 1702 (*G.*, VII, p. 504).

16. *O.F.*, pp. 86-87; 186; *N.E.*, IV, ix, §§ 3-4.

17. Cf. *N.E.*, IV, vii, § 7: "You can exclude this proposition [I am, I exist] from the number of Axioms with some reason because it is a proposition of fact, founded on an immediate experience, and not a necessary proposition, of which one sees the necessity in the immediate agreement of ideas. . . . But if an Axiom is understood more generally as an immediate or unprovable truth, one may say that this proposition, I exist, is an axiom; and in any case, one may be assured that it is a primitive truth. . . . "

18. *O.F.*, p. 183.

19. See note 2, p. 120.

20. E.G., *Monadologie*, §§ 31-36 (*G.*, VI, pp. 612-13); *Discours de métaphysique*, xiii; *T.*, p. 134; second letter to Clarke § 1; etc. In one letter Leibniz says there are two ways of knowing contingent truths: by experience, proceeding from the distinct perception of things; and by reason, proceeding from the Principle of Sufficient Reason. Perhaps this distinction could be used as a clue to the untangling of his apparently contradictory remarks concerning the first principle(s) of fact. (See *Log.*, pp. 255-56).

21. *T.*, p. 419.
22. Thus, in the *Théodicée* (*T.*, pp. 418-19) he contrasts propositions which "depend on the principle of contradiction, which makes necessary and indispensable truths" with the contingent truths which depend on the principle of sufficient reason. Leibniz evidently thinks that non-primitive truths of fact can "depend" on the "indispensable" first truths without being themselves "indispensable."
23. Cf. e.g., *N.E.*, IV, xvii, § 19. This formulation is found in several places--at least once with an addition corresponding to the law of excluded middle: "anything [quod libet] either is or is not." However the ontological formulation is notably rare than the formulation in terms of affirmation and denial: Cf. Raili Kauppi, *Ueber die Leibnizsche Logik* (Helsinki: *Acta Philosophica Fennica* (Fasc. XII), 1960), p. 81.
24. See for instance, *G.*, VII, pp. 304-305.
25. *Ibid.*, p. 303.
26. *Ibid.*, p. 305.
27. See for instance *Log.*, p. 256; Belaval, *Leibniz critique de Descartes*, p. 379.
28. *G.*, VII, p. 300.
29. This point was suggested to me by Konrad Marc-Wogau's critical examination of Kant's doctrine of analyticity ("Kant's Lehre vom Analytischen Urteil," *Theoria*, vol. XVII [1951]). See esp. pp. 142-145.
30. *Log.*, p. 387. See also pp. 23, 342, 347-48. Whether or not Couturat was right in maintaining that a predilection for the "intensional" point of view was the source of serious difficulty for Leibniz has been the subject of some debate. Cf. C.I. Lewis, *A Survey of Symbolic Logic* (New York: Dover Publications, 196), p. 14; and Nicholas Rescher, "Leibniz's Interpretation of His Logical Calculi," *Journal of Symbolic Logic*, vol. XIX (1954), pp. 1-13. Kauppi's monograph, cited above, deals in detail with this problem.
31. *Log.*, p. 23.
32. See, for instance, *Discours de métaphysique*, viii; Arnauld correspondence: *G.*, II, pp. 46, 52, 56. On the last mentioned page he

writes. "Always, in every affirmative true proposition, necessary or contingent, universal or singular, the notion of the predicate is in some manner comprehended in that of the subject; *praedicatum inest subjecto*; or else I do not know what truth is." The view expressed in this passage not only leaves the whole concept of negative truth in total obscurity, but also (as is well-known) causes Leibniz no end of difficulty in connection with his efforts to distinguish between necessary and contingent truths. For it is at best hard to see how the predicate of a proposition can be contained in the subject without the proposition being at least an implicit or virtual identity, and hence, on Leibniz' own view, a necessary truth. Leibniz, who was aware of the problem, apparently tried to resolve it by introducing a distinction between finite and infinite analyzability. This distinction, and its relation to the "identity" criterion of necessity will be treated briefly in the conclusion of this essay.

33. *N.E.*, IV, ii, § 1. Cf. *O.F.*, p. 518.
34. *N.E.*, IV, ii, § 1.
35. Leibniz occasionally uses the term "criterion" (criterium) of the principle: Cf. *G.*, VII, p. 296.
36. *Ibid.*
37. There is an enormous literature to be found in the journals on the problems posed by the incompatibles. Arthur Pap discusses these truths with some reference to Leibniz' doctrine in "Are All Necessary Truths Analytic?" *Philosophical Review*, LVIII (1949). The disparates have had less publicity. See, however, J.L. Austin, *Sense and Sensibilia* (Oxford: Clarendon Press, 1962), p. 123, n.: "It has often been thought to be a puzzle why A can't be B, if being A doesn't *entail* being not-B. But it is often just that 'A' and 'B' are brought in as, ostensively defined as, words for *different things*." Austin suggests that we need a new term, "ostensively analytic."

The question may be raised whether, if "yellowness is sweetness' is to be taken as necessarily false, a statement such as Hobbes' "virtue is blown up and down" should also be so regarded.

Leibniz, as far as I know, does not discuss any such proposition in relation to his identity criterion.

38. *N.E.*, I, i, § 18.
39. *Ibid.*
40. *Ibid.*
41. *N.E.*, I, i, § 19.
42. *Ibid.*, IV, ii, § 1.
43. *Ibid.*
44. *Ibid.*
45. *Ibid.*
46. Or perhaps as the stronger statement that there *is* a triangle which is not a trilateral, i.e., as a denial not merely of necessary coexistence but of universal coexistence. Cf. "a creature with a heart is not the same as a creature with a kidney." This might be taken as asserting either that the subject and predicate ideas are not the same (true); or that the attributes of having a heart and having a kidney are not *necessarily* connected (presumably true); or that they are not *universally* connected (presumably false). [Note added 1989: I believe this latter bit of philosophical-biological lore is mistaken, but never mind.]
47. *Essay*, IV, vi, § 10.
48. *N.E.*, IV, vi, § 10.
49. *Op. cit.*, p. 125.
50. *O.F.*, pp. 229-30; cf. *Log.*, p. 370, p. 347.
51. *G.*, III, pp. 258-59; cf. *Log.*, pp. 204-205; and Arthur Pap, *Semantics and Necessary Truth* (New Haven: Yale University Press, 1985), p. 10.
52. *G.*, VI, p. 323; cf. Russell, *Philosophy of Leibniz*, pp. 21-22.
53. See *G.*, VII, pp. 228-247. These fragments are translated by Lewis, *op. cit.*, pp. 291 ff.
54. *G.*, IV, p. 41.
55. *Loc. cit.*
56. Lewis observes that "Leibniz correctly foresaw the general character which logistic was to have and the problems it would set itself to solve. But though he caught the large outlines of the subject and actually delimited the field of work, he failed of any clear understanding of

the difficulties to be met, and he contributed comparatively little to the successful working out of details." (*Op. cit.*, p. 6.) The fragmentary and ultimately abortive character of Leibniz' efforts in the area of logistic reduction must be understood in connection with various factors, many of which relate both to his fundamental metaphysical presuppositions and his basic faith in traditional logic: e.g., the dogged insistence on the existential implications of universal propositions (cf. *Log.*, pp. 353-54, 348), and the refusal to admit that there are any propositions not reducible to the subject-predicate form (cf. Russell, *Philosophy of Leibniz*, pp. 13-14). Couturat has further provided a detailed catalogue of the difficulties Leibniz encountered in trying to develop an adequate notation for his logico-mathematical investigations (*Log.*, *passim*).

57. *Op. cit.*, pp. 7-8. For further discussion and criticism of Leibniz' reductions see Pap, *op. cit.*, pp. 10-13, and Russell, *Philosophy of Leibniz, loc. cit.*

58. See *G.*, VII, pp. 228-47; cf. Kauppi, *op. cit.*, p. 160. Also, *Log.*, pp. 321, 337, 346, 365.

59. *G.*, VII, p. 224.

60. *O.F.*, p. 235.

61. *Ibid.*, p. 230.

62. *G.*, VII, pp. 236-47.

63. Cf. *Log.*, pp. 89-102.

64. See also *G.*, VII, p. 296, where Leibniz speaks of the principle of identity as the "sole and the highest criterion of truth in abstract things."

65. Cf. Kauppi, *op. cit.*, p. 127. Here Kauppi remarks that non-identical axioms in Leibniz' calculi should be regarded as hypothetical. On pp. 121-22, however, she notes that: "Ein Axiom im strengen Sinne des Wortes ist für Leibniz eine solche Aussage, die sowohl notwendig wie nichtbeweisbar ist. Dieser Art sind nur die formalen Identitäten. . . . Prinzipiell gibt es also für Leibniz keine hypothetisch angenommenen Axiome."

66. See, for instance, Frege, *op. cit.*, pp. 2-3; Russell, *Introduction to Mathematical Philosophy*, chap. xviii; White, "*op. cit.*, pp. 129-63; W.V. Quine, "Two Dogmas of Empiricism" (in *From a Logical Point of View* [Cambridge: Harvard University Press, 1953]).

CHAPTER IV

LEIBNIZ' OPPOSITION TO CONVENTIONALISM AND HIS CONCEPTION OF DEFINITION

Leibniz, as we have seen, held that necessary truths depend on definition, in that "definitions joined with identical axioms express the principles of all demonstration."[1] The view that necessary truths are in some sense dependent on definition has come in this century to be closely associated with the view that they are arbitrary or "true by convention."[2] The conventionalistic conception of definition and of truths derived from definitions had already, however, gained a firm foothold in the seventeenth century--particularly in the works of the major English philosophers of this period, Hobbes and Locke. Leibniz found conventionalism very little to his liking, and undertook to refute it both in the course of criticizing Locke's position in the *Nouveaux Essais*, and in passages scattered throughout his other writings, directed primarily against Hobbes. His arguments against conventionalism have been widely applauded by commentators: Couturat, for instance, characterizes them as "decisive."[3] I shall argue, however, that as a refutation of conventionalism Leibniz' arguments have serious limitations, and that there is strong indication that he both misapprehended the details of the conventionalists' position, and failed to grasp the significance of their basic insight concerning the nature of definition.

1. THE CONVENTIONALISM OF HOBBES AND LOCKE

Hobbes.--Hobbes' conventionalistic conception of definition has already been noted in chapter 1. He further indicates from time to time that since definition, or the fixing of the "signification of names" is wholly arbitrary, and since scientific truths are all (as he believes) derivable from definitions alone, such truth itself must be regarded as resting entirely on human convention, and as providing no knowledge about reality, but only about the significations arbitrarily accorded to words. He writes, for instance, that in questions of human science,

> truth is sought out by natural reason and syllogisms, drawn from the covenants of men, and definitions, that is to say, significations received by use and common consent of words; such as are all questions of right and philosophy; for example, when in matter of right it is questioned, whether there be *a promise* and *covenant*, or not, that is nothing else but to demand whether such words, spoken in such a manner, be by common use and consent of the subjects a *promise* or *covenant*; which if they be so called, then it is true that a contract is made; if not, then it is false; that truth therefore depends on the compacts and consents of men.[4]

It is true that the last part of this passage seems to have to do directly not with the definition of "promise," but with the question of what is to count *as* a promise; however, Hobbes continues:

> In like manner, when it is demanded in philosophy, whether the same thing may entirely be in divers places at once; the determination of the question depends on the knowledge of the common consent of men, about the signification of the word *entire*. For if men, when they say a thing is entirely somewhere, do signify by common consent that they understand nothing of the same to be elsewhere; it is false that the same thing is in diverse places at once. That truth

therefore depends on the consents of men, and by the same reason, in all other questions concerning *right* and *philosophy*.[5]

With regard to the point that truth derived from definition will illuminate only the meanings of words, and not the nature of reality, an extreme statement may be found in Hobbes's "Fourth Objection" to the *Meditations* of Descartes:

> What shall we say, if perhaps reasoning is nothing but the copulation and concatenation of names or of appellations by the verb *is*? In this case we infer by reason nothing at all concerning the nature of things, but only about their appellations: whether or not (no doubt) we may copulate the names of the things according to an agreement [pacta] which we have arbitrarily made about their significations.[6]

It is unquestionably passages such as these which Leibniz has in mind when he takes Hobbes to task, as he so frequently does, for holding that truth "consists in names and is merely arbitrary." The following Leibnizian summary of Hobbes' position on this matter is characteristic:

> Hobbes, when he saw all truths to be demonstrable from definitions, thought even truths to be arbitrary and to consist in names, since he believed all definition to be arbitrary and verbal [nominales], in as much as giving names to things is a matter of free choice [in arbitrio est nomina rebus imponere].[7]

Consistent with Hobbes' conventionalism is his "nominalistic" position that "universal," "genus," and "species" are merely "names of names." The connection between conventionalism and the denial that universals are "real" entities is suggested in the following passage from *Concerning Body*:

> This is manifest, that *genus, species, definitions*, &c. are names of words and names only; and therefore to put *genus* and *species* for things, and *definition* for the nature of any thing, as the writers of *metaphysics* have done, is not right, seeing they be only significations of what we think of the nature of things.[8]

The traditional realist view that, e.g., the species name "man" designated a real essence which is embodied in individual men and through which they are distinguished from individuals of other species tended to be accompanied by the realist conception of definition which Hobbes opposes: i.e., by the view that definitions (rather than arbitrarily stipulating the way in which a word is to be employed) express or explain the essence designated by the definiendum, and hence are actually descriptive of one aspect of the nature of things.

Locke.--Views closely related to those of Hobbes are, as Leibniz notes in the *Nouveaux Essais*, frequently expressed by Locke. We have already observed in chapter II that Locke treats definitional statements as "trifling" and purely verbal.[9] He further emphasizes, at different points in the *Essay*, that all general ideas (such as the "ideas" of species) are "only creatures of our own making"; and that signification which general words or ideas have is "nothing but a relation that, by the mind of man is added to them."[10] This is to say that a species term, the name of a virtue, or other general term does not stand for some real essence which is independent of the human will, and which is analyzed or explained by the definition attached to the term: rather the definition, arbitrarily put together by human beings, gives signification to a term which thereby comes to apply to or be predicable of real beings:

> That then which general words signify is a *sort* of things, and each of them does that, by being a sign of an abstract idea in the mind; to which idea, as things existing are found to agree, so they come to be ranked under that name, or, which is all one, be of that sort. Whereby it is evident that the *essences* of the sorts, or . . . *species* of things are nothing else but these abstract ideas. . . . From whence it is easy to observe, that the essences of the sorts of things, and consequently, the sorting of things, is the workmanship of the understanding that abstracts and makes these general ideas.[11]

Whether or not a given entity *is* (for instance) a man will depend on whether or not it conforms to the arbitrarily created "idea" which we have arbitrarily annexed to the word "man." Truths *about* species, etc., in so far as they reflect these arbitrary definitional decisions of ours, are of course arbitrary too, and convey no "real knowledge":

> 'Every man is an animal, or living body,' is as certain a proposition as can be; but no more conducing to the knowledge of things than to say, a palfrey is an ambling horse, or a neighing, ambling animal, both being only about the signification of words, and make me know but this--That body, sense, and motion, or power of sensation and moving, are three of those ideas that I always comprehend and signify by the word man: and where they are not to be found together, the *name man* belongs not to that thing: and so of the other. ...[12]

It must be observed, however, that according to both Hobbes and Locke, definitional truths are "verbal" in the sense that they have to do with the *significations* of words, and not in the sense that they have to do merely with the sensible symbols which appear on the page. For both philosophers, moreover, the "signification" of a word is identified, at least to some extent, with an idea in the mind of the user of language. That this is true in the case of Locke is fully indicated by the passages already quoted, and is in any case sufficiently well known to require no documentation. That Hobbes held a similar view of meaning is evident, for instance, from his definition of "name":

> A NAME is a word taken at pleasure to serve for a mark, which may raise in our mind a thought like to some thought we had before, and which being pronounced to others, may be to them a sign of what thought the speaker had, or had not before in his mind.[13]

Elsewhere he emphasizes that "evidence" is essential to knowledge, and "evidence" he explains as "the concomitance of a man's *conception* with the *words* that signify such conception in the act of ratiocination. ... "[14] He remarks that "this evidence ... is meaning with our words," and further: "the truth of a proposition is never evident, until we conceive the meaning of the words or terms whereof it consisteth, which are always conceptions of the mind . . . "[15]

This aspect of the seventeenth century conventionalists' views about meaning appears to have been overlooked by Leibniz, as we shall soon see.

2. LEIBNIZ' OBJECTIONS TO CONVENTIONALISM

The need for axioms in demonstration.--It must be admitted that the fact that Leibniz holds identical axioms, as well as definitions, to be essential to demonstration of truths of reason gives him the grounds for a partial reply to Hobbes' view that *since* definitions are wholly arbitrary, derived truths must also be wholly arbitrary. For as we have already noted, it is really not clear that the principle of identity can be treated as an arbitrary decision about the use of words. If this is so, propositions derived from this principle by the substitution of definition would not be wholly arbitrary. Thus, as Leibniz in one place writes, the "convenient expression" of necessary truths "depends on definitions arbitrarily chosen," but " the truth depends on the axioms which I am accustomed to call identical."[16] This view I am not concerned to challenge. But Leibniz is not satisfied to rest his case against conventionalism here. He wants to hold further that the *only arbitrary aspect* of truths derived from axioms by means of definition is the physical symbols in which the truths happen to be expressed. The "truths themselves" are regarded as independent of the symbols,[17] and independent of the will of man.

Different words, same truth.--One point which Leibniz raises more than once to show the error of the conventionalist position that truth depending on definition is verbal, is already found in Descartes' reply to the "objection" of Hobbes which was cited above.[18] This is the observation that the *same* truth may be stated in different languages, the same mathematical proposition in different systems of notation. Thus in one place he remarks concerning the position of Hobbes:

> He affirms that truth consists in names, and, what is more, that it depends on the human will, since truths depend on the

definitions of terms, and the definitions of terms on the human
will. This is the view of a man counted among the most
profound of the age.... But nevertheless it cannot stand [stare
non potest]. As in Arithmetic, so also in other disciplines the
same truths remain even when the signs are changed, and it
does not matter whether a decimal or duodecimal progression
is employed.[19]

And in an interesting early dialogue dealing with the question of conventionalism a character to whom Hobbes' ideas have just been introduced is made to exclaim:

Surely no one can depart so far from his senses as to persuade
himself that truth is arbitrary and depends on names, when it
is certain that the geometry of the Greeks, Latins, and
Germans is the same.[20]

To which the more sophisticated speaker immediately agrees. And finally, Leibniz carries this line of argument to a logical extreme in the *Nouveaux Essais*, where he observes that if truths are to be regarded as merely verbal or distinguished by signs, there will be "truths of paper or of parchment, black truths of ordinary ink, or of printers ink."[21] This he evidently regards as a *reductio ad absurdum* of the "verbalist" positions: if truths consist in signs, any variation in the signs will entail a variation in the nature of the truth, whereas in fact many physical properties of signs expressing a "truth" have no direct bearing on what is expressed. Truth, therefore, is not to be identified with an arrangement of signs.

These considerations lead, Leibniz believes, to the conclusion that it is better "to place truth in the relation between objects of ideas, by which one is included or not included in the other."[22] Only from this point of view does it make sense to attribute truth to God, who "has no need of signs."

And when God manifests truth to us we acquire what is in his
understanding, for although there is an infinite difference
between his ideas and ours, as to perfection and breadth
[etendue], it is still true that there is agreement in the relation

[qu'on convient dans le même rapport]. It is thus in this relation that truth should be found, and we can distinguish truths, which are independent of our choice, and expressions, which we devise as we wish.[23]

From the observation that truth does not consist in physical signs, in as much as the *same* truth may be expressed by *different* combinations of signs, Leibniz thus tries to draw the conclusion that no truth should be regarded as arbitrary. But surely this reasoning is not cogent as it stands. We have already observed that neither Locke nor Hobbes held the position that "truth consists in words," according to Leibniz' literal interpretation of this expression. When these two philosophers characterize truths depending on definition as verbal and arbitrary, they do not seem at all to mean that such truths are to be construed as a mere string of uninterpreted marks (as Leibniz seems to imply). Rather they are maintaining that the truths give us no information beyond indicating or elucidating a human decision about the *signification* of words. Thus, "rational animal" and "animal doué de raison" can have the same meaning, or as Locke would say, signify the same idea, without its being any less the case, that the concept of rational animality was devised by human beings for their own purposes, and that words such as "man," "homme," etc., have arbitrarily been chosen to "signify" it.[24] The fact still remains that if "all men are rational" is a necessary truth, being derived from the definition of "man," it will be so *because* "rational" is included in the definition of "man," which inclusion is apparently a result of human choice or language-practice. Leibniz' arguments to this extent seem to leave untouched the conventionalist contention that definitional truths are arbitrary.

The apparent incompleteness of the argument from the independence of "truths" of the particular symbolism in which they are expressed, to the conclusion that definitional truths are not arbitrary may perhaps be explained by the fact that Leibniz seems simply to *assume* that if "significations," "ideas," or "conceptions" are allowed to enter the picture at all, we *must* be dealing with a wholly non-arbitrary element. He remarks, for instance (in reply to Locke's contention that complex ideas are arbitrarily put together by men): "I believe that the arbitrary [or arbitrariness] is found only in words and not at all in ideas."[25] As the passage quoted on the preceding page indicates, he seems to take it for granted that any human concept or idea is a reflection--or as he usually says, "expression"--of a pre-existent ontological reality, an idea in the mind of God. He does not seem to conceive the possibility of any middle position between the view that truth consists in uninterpreted physical marks, and the acceptance of a platonic theory of meaning.

The requirement of consistency.--Leibniz' realist conception of meaning and of definition will become clearer as we consider a further argument which he frequently brings against the conventionalists, in which this conception again figures importantly. He often argues, against Hobbes and Locke, that definitions (and truths derived by means of them) are not arbitrary, on the grounds that no expression which involves a self-contradiction may be admitted into a demonstration, for "from notions involving a contradiction, opposite conclusions may simultaneously be derived, which is absurd."[26] On this contention he erects a distinction between "real" and "nominal" definitions. A definition is "real" if it *makes known the possibility* of its subject: i.e., if it allows us to see that the subject is not intrinsically self-contradictory.

> We cannot safely use definitions to derive conclusions until we know that they are real, or involve no contradiction. . . . And thus we have . . . a way of distinguishing between *nominal definitions*, which contain only marks for distinguishing a thing from others, and *real definitions*, by which it is established that the thing is possible; and this consideration answers Hobbes, who held truths to be arbitrary, since they depended on nominal definitions, failing to observe that the reality of a definition is not a matter of choice [in arbitrio non esse], and not all notions can be joined together.[27]

The primary kind of real definition is one which presents a "complete" analysis of the definiendum into its simplest terms, revealing that there is no hidden contradiction. That the analysis offered in the definiens is complete and that no two of the ultimate terms are incompatible is something which must be perceived by intuition. These perfect intuitive real definitions are, at best, rare.[28] But there are, according to Leibniz, other ways in which a definition can show that the concept denoted by the definiendum is "possible"--e.g., by showing how to create an object corresponding to this concept. For instance, a geometrical definition of a figure can express a means for constructing that figure: but if a figure can be constructed, it must be "possible." Therefore, such a definition makes known the possibility of its subject.[29] Leibniz apparently does not want to call the knowledge of possibility gained through these "causal" real definitions "intuitive."[30] He emphasizes, however, that "every real definition contains at least some affirmation of possibility."[31] He further concedes that *nominal* definitions may be used in demonstration when the possibility of the definiendum has been "established by other means"--i.e., by *experience* of the existence of an object corresponding to the idea defined, "for what actually exists or has existed is at any rate possible."[32]

Leibniz believes that the fact that an apprehension of possibility is required before a definition is admitted to a demonstration constitutes a complete refutation of conventionalism,[33] and many commentators, as noted above, seem to agree with him. For the admissibility of a definition can no longer be regarded as resting on human decision: it rather depends on the *discovery* that what we are trying to express by definition is "possible":

> Thus it does not depend on us to join ideas however we please, unless this combination is justified either by reason, which shows it to be possible, or by experience, which shows it to be actual, and consequently possible as well.[34]

Now Leibniz might be challenged on the point that the requirement of "possibility" or self-consistency introduces a restriction on the creation of definition which is unavoidable and independent of the human will. It might be suggested, for instance, that it is *up to us* whether propositions derived from definitions involving impossibilities are to be admitted as truths or not: e.g., whether it is to be admitted as true that "round squares have angles," even though one can equally well deduce from the "impossible notion" of a round square that "round squares have no angles." It is particularly interesting, in this connection, that in one of his sketches of a calculus Leibniz himself defines as *true* any proposition which may be proved by the axioms of the calculus and definitions, and puts no restriction on the choice of definitions--i.e., self-contradictory definitions are not excluded. A derived proposition such as "A square circle is a quadrangle with no angles" is to be counted as a "propositio vera ex hypothese impossibile."[35]

However, even if it is *accepted* that definitions must be self-consistent, this would appear to entail only a *limitation* on the arbitrariness of definition. It would *not* seem to establish that truths dependent on definition--i.e., all necessary truths apart from the express identities--are not in any significant sense arbitrary. For surely there still remains a wide scope for the exercise of choice in creating definitions. For instance, "all men are rational" will be a necessary truth if and only if "rational" is included in the definition of "man"--and whether or not it is so included will still appear to be a matter of arbitrary choice, as long as it is assumed that the notion of rationality is not self-contradictory, and that no other element in the definition of "man" entails "non-rational." Thus while the requirement of self-consistency may, if accepted, *limit* our invention of "general ideas," or definitions of terms, it does not seem to entail that these ideas or definitions are not invented by us. Leibniz, however, clearly believes that it does.

The reason why Leibniz regards the restriction to possible concepts as a reply to conventionalism is apparently identical with his reason for insisting (in general) on the exclusive "reality" of definitions which make known the possibility of their concepts. It is to be found in his *ontological* view that possible concepts and only possible concepts are real essences, which have an eternal, prelinguistic subsistence in the mind of God. On this account, any concept susceptible of a "real definition"--i.e., any non-self-contradictory concept--will have "always existed" as an object of God's thought, and hence *cannot* be created by man:

> Whether men join certain ideas [telles ou telles idées] or not, and even whether nature joins them in actuality or not; that is irrelevant with respect to the essences, genera, or species, since

>it is here not a question of anything except the possibilities which are independent of our thought.[36]

The view that all "possibles" are eternal and real seems actually to be a premise of Leibniz' philosophical system. It cannot in any sense be regarded as a consequence of his theology, since he rather argues *from* the "eternal reality" of possibles to the conclusion that they must be "grounded" in some eternal actuality or existent--i.e in the mind of God. It is not at all clear why it should not be open to the conventionalist to challenge or simply to reject Leibniz' ontology.

But even if it is *agreed* that possible concepts and only possible concepts have the platonic status of "real ideas," it does not seem to follow that truths which depend on definition are not, in an important sense, arbitrary. For it is still the case that human beings, in providing definitions for terms, select, as it were, various possible concepts and reject others. And which truths are necessary will depend not on which concepts are real in Leibniz' sense, but rather on which ones are selected by human beings to enter into the formation of language. For instance, whether "all men are rational" is a necessary truth or not will depend on whether or not "rational" *has been made* part of the definition of "man"; if "All men are mortal" is not necessarily true it will still be because "man" has not been defined with reference to mortality, or to some concept entailing mortality. Similarly, what creatures *are men* will still depend, it would seem, on what sorts of creatures we have agreed to *count as* "men." No consideration seems to have been advanced that would constitute a refutation of Locke's point that to "be a man" is nothing more nor less than to be rightly called "a man," where "rightly" can only mean "in accordance with human conventions dictating how the word "man" is to be applied."

It might be thought that when Leibniz maintains that truths are not arbitrary, he means *no more* than that we are restricted in creating definitions by the necessity of conforming to the principle of non-contradiction, and that hence we do not strictly "create' them at all, but merely use them to express or select pre-existing possibles, and to "attach" the possible selected to certain words. On this view, however, *definitional truths* would still be created by us, in as much as the proposition "All men are rational" would (as already observed) be (necessarily) true merely *because* we had selected the possible concept "rational animal" and *made it the definition* of "man." And that truths are arbitrary in this way Leibniz is not prepared to admit. He repeatedly, in fact, characterizes necessary truths as eternal and as known by God, "who has no need of signs."

The heart of the matter seems to be this. When Leibniz speaks of a possible concept or real essence he is not usually thinking of just any combination or two or more compatible "simple ideas," but rather of something much nearer a real essence in the traditional sense. In respect of the definition of "man," the point is not that "rational animal" and "featherless biped" equally denote possible concepts and hence are equally eligible to become definitions of a term. Rather, there is, in Leibniz' view, a perfect concept of the species *man* which exists in God's mind from eternity, and of which the *existing species* is an "expression," or from which it "emanates."[37] Our *definitions* of "man" must actually be regarded as partial and more or less adequate expressions of God's perfect concept.[38] Thus "rational animal" and "featherless biped" do not constitute--as might be supposed--*two different possible concepts*, but rather express the same "possibility" from different "points of view."

> In order ... to distinguish Essence and definition, it is necessary to consider that there is only one essence of anything, but there are several definitions which express the same essence [une même essence], as the same structure or the same city can be represented by different Scenographs, according to the different sides from which one looks at it.[39]

> The same subject can have several definitions, but to know that they pertain to the same thing [conviennent au même], one must learn it by reason, in demonstrating one definition by the other; or by experience, in proving that they always go together [vont constamment ensemble].[40]

In regard to existing species, we strive to "express" or explain through our definition the essence or "interior nature" which constitutes the species.[41]

Thus Leibniz sometimes says that definitions are, as a rule, merely provisional: as our knowledge of the concept or species which we are trying to define becomes more adequate, or as we approach an understanding of its "interior nature," the definition is also improved or brought up to date.[42] He accordingly characterizes Plato's definition of "man" (featherless biped with broad nails) as "manifestly a little too external, and too provisional." For, he remarks, if a sort of bird previously described by Locke as having a hairlike covering rather than ordinary feathers, should turn out to have broad nails, it would, on Plato's definition, be a man.[43] Reason, on the other hand, is an *essential* attribute of the species, man; he also speaks of "necessary" connections among the properties of a substance.[44] If we are dealing with a "monster," which species it belongs to--i.e., what essence or internal nature it possesses--is, he says, a matter of conjecture.[45]

All this, I submit, far from constituting a "decisive" refutation of Hobbesian and Lockean conventionalism, appears to indicate that Leibniz has failed to apprehend the basic issue. As Locke, in particular, makes clear, the problem is that if a general term is to have "signification," there must be a *criterion* for its application; the role of a definition is, according to the conventionalists, simply to provide such a criterion. But it is nonsense to say that a criterion is accurate or inaccurate, adequate or inadequate: it is merely a stipulation (and to this extent fundamentally arbitrary). In determining the scope or extension of a general term, moreover, the definition *thereby determines* a species. Until we have a criterion for the application of a general term, there cannot be (on the conventionalist view) any "species" corresponding to that term. Further, once the general term is defined, the species is *ipso facto* completely determined. If "man" is defined as "rational animal," to be a man is neither more nor less than to be a rational animal. Although God may have a more complete knowledge than we do of additional characteristics in fact possessed by existing rational animals, it is nonsense to speak of his having more complete knowledge of what it is "to be a man." This would be exactly like saying that he alone has complete knowledge of the absence of bachelorhood, whereas we merely provisionally define "bachelor" as "unmarried man," until we can find out more about what bachelorhood consists in.

Leibniz sometimes supports his contention that the division of reality into sorts of species is not arbitrary with the observation that there are real resemblances in things.[46] He appears to overlook Locke's explanation that his point is not really material, since *which* resemblances are to constitute the basis for the determination of species is still a matter of human decision:

> I would not here be thought to forget, much less to deny, that Nature, in the production of things, makes several of them alike: there is nothing more obvious . . . .But yet I think we may say, *the sorting of them under names is the workmanship of the understanding, taking occasion, from the similitude it observes amongst them, to make abstract general ideas*, and set them up in the mind, with names annexed to them, as patterns or forms . . . to which as particular things existing are found to agree, so they come to be of that species, have that denomination, or are put in that *classis*.[47]

The marginal summary of this section of the *Essay* reads as follows: "[Abstract ideas which are the Essences of Genera and Species] are the Workmanship of the Understanding, but have their Foundation in the Similitude of Things." It is evidence, I believe, of Leibniz' superficial reading of Locke, that he picks up only the last clause of this summary, putting into the mouth of Locke's advocate the statement, "I was going to tell you myself that these species are founded on resemblances." To which his man replies, "Then why not also look for the essence of genera and Species in resemblances?"[48] Locke's point is that the fact that human beings are apt to define their terms in a way which reflects existing resemblances and dissimilarities in nature, in human actions, etc., does not at all entail that a definition should be regarded as a description rather than a criterion.

Leibniz, then, does not directly meet the conventionalists' contention that definitions are fundamentally stipulative, and that accordingly truths dependent on definitions are "arbitrary" in a significant sense, but merely reasserts the traditional conception of real kinds against which these arguments are directed. His repudiation of conventionalism cannot, therefore, be regarded as in any way conclusive. I do not wish to deny, however, that some aspects of his anti-conventionalist position might be susceptible of a more compelling defense than he in fact supplies. It could perhaps be pointed out, for instance, that general terms are frequently "defined" *ostensively*, rather than by the verbal statement of a criterion for their application. A verbal definition might afterwards be arrived at through a conceptual or empirical analysis of the characteristics of those objects which are (somehow) recognized through the ostensive definition as falling under the extension of the term in question. Thus, we may all learn to recognize human beings without having been told in so many words what a human being *is*. As we become more philosophical, the argument would continue, we begin to ask ourselves precisely what salient features these various entities have in common, which we have implicitly been using as cues in classing them all together under the term "human being." And it might turn out that two who could be held to have (roughly) the same concept of human-being-ness, on the grounds that they immediately recognized (roughly) the same entities as human beings, nevertheless, come up with different "definitions" of "human being." In this way, two definitions might after all be said to "express the same concept." Also, one definition might be judged more "adequate" than the other, on the grounds that it was more in conformity with our "intuitive" pre-analytical conception of what something would have to be like to be counted a human being. Even this picture of the enterprise of definition, however, would not appear to clarify the Leibnizian view that rationality is necessarily connected with humanity in some non-arbitrary way.

We have so far been considering the problem of definition primarily in relation to species-concepts. Leibniz, of course, regards his theory of definition as the "expression" of eternal ideas as embracing mathematical concepts as well. He maintains, for instance, that both physical circles and our idea of circle or circularity are "expressions" of an eternal archetype of this figure existing in the intellect of God.[49] (Our idea of circularity, as opposed to our idea of humanity, he takes to be innate.[50]) Although, for purposes of demonstration, we endeavor to express this essence in the most convenient symbolic form, the truths which we demonstrate are not merely verbal, but rather truths "about" the eternal essences involved.[51] The "reality" of mathematical truths is again *established* by reference to the need for an intuition of possibility.[52] And again it does not seem that the requirement of "possibility" actually does establish (against Locke's denial) that mathematical ideas have a "source" independent of the human will.

3. LEIBNIZ' CONCEPTION OF DEFINITION AND HIS DOCTRINE OF NECESSITY

Aside from the success or unsuccess of Leibniz' opposition to conventionalism, his views about definition suggest some problems or questions when considered in relation to his doctrine of necessary truth. In the first place, it should by now be clear that his theory can be called "objective" and "formalistic" only in a quite limited sense. Although reduction to a formal principle by means of definition expressed in "palpable" signs is required to establish a proposition as necessarily true, the admissibility and satisfactoriness of the definitions themselves are, it would seem, to be decided on intuitive grounds. Leibniz sometimes remarks that it does not matter what definitions we start with in setting up a characteristic by means of which truths are to be demonstrated, "since all will lead to the same result as the resolution is continued."[53] It is not at all clear why this should be so, however; and elsewhere Leibniz emphasizes the need for "good" definitions.[54] Further, in the *Nouveaux Essais* he discounts a "demonstration" which Locke offers of a political or ethical proposition ("There cannot be injustice where there is no property.") on the grounds that one of the definitions which Locke employs is not acceptable.[55] It is hard to see why the disputes and the uncertainty which Leibniz hopes to eliminate by insisting on demonstration should not be expected to reappear when it comes to the important matter of deciding on definitions.[56] With regard to mathematical demonstrations, it appears that Leibniz does not regard it as nonsensical to suppose that there could be materially different opinions concerning, say, the nature of a circle, since he writes to a correspondent that "the nature of the circle with its properties is something existent and eternal: i.e., there is a cause outside of us which makes it the case that all who think of the circle carefully, discover the same thing

. . . ."[57] One might also question whether an anti-reductionist such as Descartes or Locke could not simply reject Leibniz' contention that "three and one" is "the definition" of "four," on the grounds that according to *his* intuition, "four" is an indefinable and simple notion.

One further difficulty may be mentioned. As we have noted, Leibniz holds that the primary kind of real definition is one which presents a complete analysis of its concept down to the primitive terms out of which it is constituted, thus making possible an "intuition" of the possibility of that concept. The question arises, under what circumstances can a concept turn out to be *impossible*. It would appear that this can only occur when there is an "incompatibility" among the primitive ideas. But can the incompatibility of primitive ideas be formal or "analytic"? Apparently not, since formal incompatibility involves negation; and since a primitive concept is a concept which is understood through itself,"[58] what appears to be precluded is, precisely, its being understood through its relation to other primitive concepts. It follows that a primitive concept cannot be understood as a negation or opposite of some other concept.[59] Apparently, then, it is a consequence of Leibniz' theory of definition that there are ultimate incompatibilities which are not formal (or based on the principle of non-contradiction), but "synthetic."[60] Indeed, Leibniz' emphasis on the crucial role played by *intuition* in deciding on the possibility or impossibility of the concept defined seems to constitute a tacit admission that incompatibility may be non-formal, since formal incompatibilities (contradictions) are *demonstrated* rather than "intuited." We have already noted, however, that Leibniz' treatment in the *Nouveaux Essais* of such propositions as "what is white is not black" seems to commit him to the position that there are incompatibilities and necessary connections which cannot be formally demonstrated. Consideration of his view concerning definition only serves to confirm the point that there are severe limitation to his ability to carry through a "formalistic" theory of necessity.

NOTES

1. *N.E.*, IV, viii, § 12.
2. See, for instance, Ayer, *op. cit.*, chap. iv, esp. pp. 79 and 82.
3. *Log.*, 103. Cf. H.W.B. Joseph, *Lectures on the Philosophy of Leibniz* (Oxford: Clarendon Press, 1949), p. 92.
4. English Works, ed. Molesworth (hereafter "E.W."), vol. II, pp. 295-296.
5. *Ibid.*
6. Thomas Hobbes, *Opera philosophica quae latine scripsit omnia*, ed. William Molesworth (reprint of ed. 1839-45; Scientia Aalen, 1961), vol. V, pp. 257-58. The second sentence is somewhat oddly constructed in the original Latin. I assume that the clause following the colon explains *what* we infer about names through reason and have translated accordingly.
7. *G.*, VII, pp. 294-95.
8. I, ii, § 10.
9. Of course Locke does not share Hobbes' view that "all of scientific knowledge" is based on mere definition. In fact, Locke does not even believe that all necessary truth depends on definition: the important truths which are "self-evident" but non-trifling do not.
10. *Essay*, III, iii, §§ 11-13. Locke holds, however, that general terms are compounded out of "simple ideas" and that simple ideas are not invented by men but derived from sense experience or reflection. It is therefore strictly only the *combination* that is arbitrary. Cf. e.g. *Essay*, III, iv, § 17, and vi, § 21.
11. *Ibid.*, § 12. Cf. III, vi, § 7.
12. *Ibid.*, IV, viii, § 6.
13. *Concerning Body*, I, ii, § 4. As Peters remarks (*Hobbes*, p. 127-28; cf. 133), however, Hobbes' position differs from Locke's in that Hobbes does not believe that the "conceptions" which are associated with words are properly regarded as "general" or "universal." He seems rather to hold that the meaning of a general term is found in the

"several" conceptions in our mind of different particular individuals to which the term is applicable (Cf. *Concerning Body*, I, ii, § 9.

14. E.W., IV, p. 28.
15. *Ibid*.
16. *G.*, I, p. 369. Cf. *Log.*, pp. 187-88. A similar point seems to be in question at *G.*, VII, p. 193, where it is observed that although terms are arbitrary, a "certain order or rule" must be followed in using them in demonstrations, which remains constant even when the characters are varied. See also *G.*, VII, p. 219.
17. Leibniz repeatedly asserts, however, that thought is impossible for human beings without the employment of some set of signs or other. See, e.g., *G.*, VII, p. 191.
18. The reply is printed following the objection in the *Opera omnia* of Hobbes. See above, p. 152, n.1.
19. *G.*, IV, p. 158.
20. *G.*, VII, p. 191.
21. IV, v, § 1.
22. *N.e., loc. cit.*
23. *Ibid*.
24. Hobbes, in fact, devotes a section of *Concerning Body* to the topic, "the same proposition diversely pronounced." It begins, "But seeing every proposition may be, and uses to be, pronounced and written in many forms. . . . " (I, iii, § 12.)
25. *N.E.*, III, iv, § 17.
26. *G.*, IV, p. 424.
27. *Ibid.*, pp. 424-25.
28. See, e.g., *G.*, IV, p. 425.
29. *G.*, VII, p. 294.
30. cf. *G.*, IV, pp. 423-24; *N.E.*, iv, ii, § 1; *G.*, VII, 295.
31. *G.*, VII, p. 295.
32. *G.*, IV, p. 425.
33. The point that "this consideration answers Hobbes" (or conventionalism generally) is made over and over again by Leibniz.

Besides the passage already cited see *Discours de métaphysique*, xxiv (*G.*, IV, p. 450); *N.E.*, IV, viii, § 12.
34. *N.E.*, III, iii, § 15.
35. See *G.*, VII, pp. 219-25, and Kauppi, *op. cit.*, pp. 158-159.
36. *N.E.*, III, iii, § 14.
37. Cf. *N.E.*, III, vi, 39; *O. F.*, p. 513; *G.*, IV, p. 425; also Belaval, *Leibniz critique de Descartes*, p. 155.
38. Cf. *G.*, II, p. 131: "Can it be denied that each thing (whether genus, species or individual) has a complete notion [notion accomplie], according to which God conceives it, who conceives everything perfectly, i.e., a notion which includes or comprehends everything which one can say about the thing . . . ."
39. *N.E.*, III, iii, § 15.
40. *Ibid.*, xi, §§ 11-21.
41. *Ibid.*, §22; iii, § 18, etc.
42. *Ibid.*, III, *passim*: e.g., vi, § 34.
43. *Ibid.*, x, §§ 17-18.
44. *Ibid.*, vi, § 35; cf. vi, § 4.
45. *Ibid.*, vi, §§ 14-16.
46. See, for instance, *N.E.*, III, vi, § 32; iii, § 12.
47. *Essay*, III, iii, § 13. The italics are in the text.
48. *N.E.*, III, iii, § 13.
49. Cf. *N.E.*, II, xxxii, § 3; Belaval, *Leibniz critique de Descartes*, pp. 141-42.
50. Cf *N.E.*, I, i, § 18, § 23.
51. Cf. *G.*, VII, p 305.
52. Cf. *N.E.*, IV, ii, § 13.
53. *Math. Schrift.* (gerhardt), IV, p. 462.
54. Cf., e.g., *Log.*, p. 281, n.
55. *N.E.*, IV, iii, § 18.
56. Hobbes, who was also concerned with the value of demonstration for settling disputes and controversies, perceived that it was not unlikely that this should occur, and accordingly decreed that when a controversy arose concerning signification or definition, the matter

was to be settled by the city government! See E.W., II, pp. 268-69, and Peters, *op. cit.*, pp. 54-55, 60.
57. *G.*, I, p. 370.
58. *G.*, VII, p. 293.
59. Leibniz was himself troubled by the question of how primitive or simple ideas could be incompatible. Cf. *G.*, VII, p. 195. See also *Log.*, p. 432.
60. This point was originally made by Russell (cf. *Philosophy of Leibniz*, pp. 17-18), and has been reiterated by other commentators, including Pap and Joseph. But it seems desirable, in the present context, to enunciate it once more.

CONCLUSION

We have now considered from various points of view Leibniz' doctrine that a *necessary* truth is a proposition which can be reduced to a formal identity by the substitution of definitions. We have seen to what extent this doctrine may correctly be called "traditional," and to what extent, on the other hand, it must be regarded as involving an important and interesting advance over traditional conceptions. We have examined in some detail Leibniz' efforts to vindicate the enterprise of reduction in opposition to the intuitionism of Descartes and Locke, and we have noted his emphasis, in arguing against these contemporaries, on the value of his doctrine in providing a formal and objective method for the demonstration of "truths of reason." It has been found, however, that Leibniz does not consistently maintain the view that "necessity" may be *defined* solely in terms of the criterion of formal identity, since he wishes also to say that the principle of identity or non-contradiction is itself necessary in the sense of being an indispensable condition of rational discourse. We have also learned that there are severe limitations on Leibniz' ability to carry through and to support his contention that all necessary truths are express or implicit identities. Propositions such as "the white is not the black" are treated by Leibniz as necessary, but he is evidently not capable of establishing that they are true by the principle of non-contradiction. Further, while he repeatedly *asserts* that all of mathematics may be reduced to the principle of non-contradiction or identity, he makes relatively little progress in *showing* that this is the case. It follows that he would not be in a position to answer either the contention of certain recent writers that "the white is not the black," for instances, is an example of a *synthetic* necessary truth; or the view of such modern logisticists as Frege and Russell that the principle of non-contradiction has "no special pre-eminence" among logical truths.[1] Finally, we have found that Leibniz' efforts to establish against the conventionalists that necessary truths, although dependent on definition, are not arbitrary, are by no means wholly successful or convincing; and we have noted that his conception of definition seems both to involve the admission of an important "subjective" element in the demonstration of necessary truths, and to require recognition of the existence of "synthetic" or non-formal incompatibilities.

In conclusion, I would like to take note of a contention found in the writings of many of Leibniz' commentators that he did not really regard "reducibility to the principle of non-contradiction" as providing the basis for the definition of "necessary truth", except in a very qualified sense. This rather paradoxical notion is strongly suggested by the fact, mentioned in chapter iii, that Leibniz' repeatedly remarks that in *all* true affirmative propositions the predicate is "in some way" contained in the concept of the subject. For it is at best hard to see how the predicate of a proposition can be contained in the subject without the proposition being at least an implicit or virtual identity. But this would lead to the conclusion that necessary and contingent truths are alike identities.[2]

Leibniz, who was aware of the problem, apparently attempted to resolve it by introducing a distinction between finite and infinite analyzability. Necessary truths are those in respect of which the containment of the predicate in the subject may be demonstrated by a finite number of steps; whereas the analysis of the subject of contingent truths proceeds to infinity (and hence the truth of such propositions may be known a priori only by God).[3] Now, the important and difficult question is whether Leibniz regarded this criterion or definition of necessity as *superseding* or as *complementing* the definition in terms of non-contradiction. That is, did Leibniz, or did he not, wish to hold that truths demonstrable by "infinite analysis," as well as those demonstrable by "finite analysis," are true by identity?[4] Many of his critics (Dewey,[5] Russell after reading Couturat,[6] Gottfried Martin) have assumed that he did, and there are indeed a number of passages in his writings which very clearly support this interpretation:

> The *first truths* . . . can all be grouped under the one name of *identities*. All other truths may be reduced to the first truths by definitions, or by the resolution of the notions . . . .

> Therefore the predicate or consequent is always contained in the subject or antecedent. And in this fact consists the nature of truth in general . . . . These considerations . . . give rise to the accepted maxim that *nothing is without reason* . . . . Otherwise there would be truth which . . . could not be resolved into identicals, which is opposed to the nature of truth, which is always either expressly or implicitly identical.[7]

Other passages, however, just as clearly suggest that he did *not* regard truths "demonstrable" by infinite analysis as true by identity or non-contradiction. In discussion the problem of distinguishing necessary from contingent truths, he remarks:

> I say that it is common to all affirmative true propositions--both universal and singular, necessary or contingent, that the predicate is in the subject, or that the notion of the predicate is in some sense involved in the notion of the subject . . . . But this observation seemed only to increase the difficulty for if the notion of the predicate, at any given time, is contained in the notion of the subject, how can this predicate ever be removed from [abesse] the subject without contradiction or impossibility.[8]

He goes on to say that there are two classes of (non-primitive) truths: some can be reduced to identities, and are necessary; the others "admit a resolution *in infinitum*," and are contingent. He continues: "A necessary proposition is one of which the opposite implies a contradiction . . . ." In contingent truths, however,

> even though the predicate is contained in the subject, nevertheless no demonstration of this is possible, and the proposition can never be reduced to an equation or an identity, but the resolution proceeds *in infinitum*, God alone seeing, not indeed the end of the resolution, which does not exist [qui nullus est], but rather the connexion of the terms, or the

involvement of the predicate in the subject, since he sees whatever is contained in the series.[9]

This passage, and others like it,[10] seem to indicate that Leibniz wished to regard the distinction between finite and infinite analyzability as supplementing or clarifying, rather than replacing, the identity criterion. In other words, they seem to imply that he took the notion of infinite analyzability to provide the means of *reconciling* the view that in *all* truths the subject is contained in the predicate with the view that only *necessary* truths are derivable from the principle of identity. And, in fact, to the very end of his career, he was still insisting on the identity criterion as providing *in itself* adequate grounds for the necessary-contingent distinction.[11]

I think it must therefore be concluded that the widely-held view that Leibniz was committed to the position that "all truths are identities and are known by God as identities,"[12] must be regarded as at best a half-truth. Leibniz *sometimes* seems to be maintaining this thesis; at other times he expressly maintains the exact opposite. But by the same token, the contention which is occasionally brought forward in opposition to Russell and others, that Leibniz did wish to uphold a radical distinction between necessary and contingent truths, based on the principle of non-contradiction, must be received with caution.[13] It seems obviously futile to engage in further controversy about which position Leibniz held, when there is evidence is black and white that he did not hold *either* position consistently. A more fruitful topic for future discussion might be the question of what, precisely, Leibniz could mean when he speaks of God's discovering the "containment" of predicate in subject by a process of "infinite analysis."

NOTES

1. Russell, *Introduction to Mathematical Philosophy*, p. 203. In *Principia Mathematica* the principle of identity is not, in fact, treated as a primitive.
2. Leibniz never abandons the view that there *are* contingent truths.
3. Cf., e.g. *O.F.*, pp. 1, 408, etc.
4. The view that the "complete notion" of the subject of propositions which we enunciate may be apprehended by God and not by us, is, of course, closely bounded up with Leibniz' contention that our definitions are only "expressions" of God's perfect concepts.
5. In *Leibniz's New Essays Concerning the Human Understanding* (Chicago: Scott, Foresman and Co., 1902).
6. "Recent Work in the Philosophy of Leibniz," *Mind*, III (1903).
7. *O.F.*, pp. 518-519.
8. *Nouvelles lettres et opuscules inédits de Leibniz*, ed. A. Foucher de Careil (Paris: Auguest Durand, 1857), p. 179.
9. *Ibid.*, p. 182.
10. See, for instances, *G.*, VII, pp. 300-301.
11. Cf. *Monadologie*, §§ 31-36, 46; *G.*, VI, 612, etc. Russell suggests (*loc. cit.*, pp. 185-86) that Leibniz held this doctrine *only* in his later years, when he had "forgotten the reasons" for his system. But the passages cited on the proceeding pages are not late works.
12. Rulon Wells, "Leibniz Today," (Part II), *Review of Metaphysics*, X (1956-57), p. 508.
13. See, for instance, Nicholas Rescher, "Contingence in the Philosophy of Leibniz," *Philosophical Review*, LXI (1952).

BIBLIOGRAPHY*

Anscombe, G.E.M. and P.T. Geach. *Three Philosophers*. Ithaca: Cornell University Press, 1961.

Aristotle. The Basic Works. Ed. Richard McKeon. New York: Random House, 1941.

_____. *Categories and De Interpretatione*. Trans. and ed. J.L. Ackrill. Oxford: Clarendon Press, 1963.

_____. Metaphysics. Ed. W.D. Ross. Oxford: Clarendon Press, 1958.

_____. *Prior and Posterior Analytics*. Ed. W.D. Ross. Oxford: Clarendon Press, 1958.

_____. *Topica et Sophistici Elenchi*. Ed. W.D. Ross. Oxford: Clarendon Press, 1958.

Austin, J.L. *Sense and Sensibilia*. Oxford: Clarendon Press, 1962.

Ayer, A.J. *Language, Truth and Logic*. 2d ed. revised, New York: Dover, n.d.

Belaval, Yvon. *Leibniz critique de Descartes*. Paris: Librarie Gallimard, 1960.

_____. *Leibnitz: initiation à sa philosophie*. Paris: J. Vrin, 1962.

Bochenski, I.M. *A History of Formal Logic*. Trans. and ed. Ivan Thomas. Notre Dame: University of Notre Dame Press, 1961.

Cantor, Moritz. *Vorlesungen über Geschichte der Mathematik*. Leipzig: B.G. Teubner, 1880-1901.

Descartes, René. *Correspondance*. Ed. C. Adam and G. Milhaud. Paris: Presses Universitaires de France, 1960.

_____. *Oeuvres*. Ed. C. Adam et Paul Tannery. Paris: Leopold Cerf, 1897-1910.

---

*N.B.: This list is not intended as a comprehensive bibliography of the subject. It includes only works which are referred to in the text, or which contributed significantly at some point to the development of the thesis. Books listed under "Abbreviations" at the head of the text are omitted.

_____. *The Philosophical Works.* Trans. E.S. Haldane and G.R.T. Ross. New York: Dover, 1955.

Dewey, John. *Leibniz's New Essays Concerning the Human Understanding.* Chicago: Scott, Foreman, 1902.

Fischer, Kuno. *Geschichte der neuern Philosophie.* Heidelberg: Carl Winter, 1889. Vol. II.

Frege, Gottlob. *The Foundations of Arithmetic.* Trans. J.L. Austin. 2d ed. revised. New York: Harper and Bros., 1960.

_____. Translations from the Philosophical Writings. Ed. P. Geach and M. Black. Oxford: Basil Blackwell, 1960.

Geulincx, Arnold. *Opera Philosophica.* Ed. J.P.N. Land. Hague:: Martin Nyhoff, 1891.

Gilson, Etienne. *The Christian Philosophy of St. Thomas Aquinas.* Trans. L.K. Shook. New York: Random House, 1956.

Hobbes, Thomas. *The English Works.* Ed. William Molesworth. London: John Bohn, 1839.

_____. *The Leviathan.* Oxford: Clarendon Press, 1958.

_____. *Opera Philosophica quae Latini scripait omnia.* Ed. William Molesworth. Scientia Aalen, 1961.

Huber, Kurt. *Leibniz.* München: R. Oldenbourg, 1951.

Joseph, H.W.B. *Lectures on the Philosophy of Leibniz.* Oxford: Clarendon Press, 1949.

Jungius, Joachim. *Logica Hamburgensis.* Ed. Rudolf W. Meyer. Hamburg: J.J. Augustin, 1957.

Kauppi, Raili. *Ueber die Leibnizsche Logik.* Helsinki: *Acta Philosophica Fennica* (Fasc. XII), 1960.

Kneale, William and Martha. *The Development of Logic.* Oxford: Clarendon Press, 1962.

Knowles, David. *The Evolution of Medieval Thought.* Baltimore: Helicon Press, 1962.

Leibniz, G.W. *Discours de métaphysique et correspondance avec Arnauld.* Ed. Georges Le Roy. Paris: J. Vrin, 1957.

---. *The Leibniz-Clarke Correspondence.* Ed. H.G. Alexander. Manchester: Manchester University Press, 1956.

---. *Mathematische Schriften.* Ed. C.J. Gerhardt. Berlin-Halle: Ascher; Schimidt, 1849-1863.

---. *Nouveaux essais sur l'entendement humain.* Ed. Emile Boutroux. Paris: Ch. Delagrave, 1886.

---. *Philosophical Papers and Letters.* Ed. Leroy Loemker. Chicago: University of Chicago Press, 1956.

Lewis, C.I. *A Survey of Symbolic Logic.* New York: Dover, 1960.

Locke, John. *An Essay Concerning Human Understanding.* Ed. A.C. Fraser. New York: Dover, 1959.

Loemker, Leroy. "Boyle and Leibniz." *Journal of the History of Ideas*, XVI (1955).

---. "Leibniz' Judgements of Fact." *Journal of the History of Ideas*, VII (1946).

Lovejoy, A.O. *The Great Chain of Being.* Cambridge: Harvard University Press, 1957.

Marc-Wogau, Konrad. "Kant's Lehre vom analytischen Urteil." *Theoria*, XVII (1951).

Martin, Gottfried. *Leibniz: Logic and Metaphysics.* Trans. K.J. Northcott and P.G. Lucas. Manchester: Manchester University Press, 1964.

Miller, Leonard G. "Descartes, Mathematics, and God." *Philosophical Review*, LXVI (1957).

Moore, G.E. *Principia Ethica.* Cambridge: Cambridge University Press, 1959.

Nicholas of Autrecourt. *Nicolaus von Autrecourt: sein Leben, seine Philosophie, sein Schriften.* Ed. J. Lappe (*Beiträge zur Geschichte der Philosophie des Mittelalters*, Bd. II, Heft 2). Münster: Aschendorff, 1908.

[Nicole and Arnauld]. *Logique de Port-Royal.* Ed. Charles Jourdain. Paris: L. Hachette, 1854.

Pap, Arthur. "Are All Necessary Propositions Analytic?" *Philosophical Review*, LVIII (1949).

---. *Semnatics and Necessary Truth.* New Haven: Yale University Press, 1958.

Peters, Richard. *Hobbes.* Penguin Books, 1956.

Prenant, Lucy."Le raisonable chez Leibniz: la revanche du jugement sur la forme." *Revue Philosophique de la France et de L'Etranger*, CXXXVI (1946).

Quine, W.V. *From a Logical Point of View*. Cambridge: Harvard University Press, 1953.

Rescher, Nicholas. "Contingence in the Philosophy of Leibniz." *Philosophical Review*, LXI (1954).

_____. "Leibniz's Interpretation of His Logical Calculi." *Journal of Symbolic Logic*, XIX (1954).

Russell, Bertrand. *A Critical Exposition of the Philosophy of Leibniz*. London: George Allen and Unwin, 1937.

_____. *Introduction to Mathematical Philosophy*. London: George Allen and Unwin, 1919.

_____. "Recent Work in the Philosophy of Leibniz." *Mind*, XII (1903).

Ross, W.D. *Aristotle*. New York: Meridian Books, 1959.

Saame, Otto. *Der Satz vom Grund bei Leibniz*. Mainz: Hannskrach, 1961.

Saw, Ruth Lydia. *Leibniz*. Penguin Books, 1954.

Schrecker, Paul. "Leibniz et le principe du tiers exclu." *Actes du Congrés International de Philosophie Scientifique*, VI (1936).

Shapiro, Herman (ed). *Medieval Philosophy*. New York: Modern Library, 1964.

Smith, Norman Kemp. *New Studies in the Philosophy of Descartes*. London: Macmillan, 1952.

Thomas Aquinas. *Commentary on the Metaphysics of Aristotle*. Trans. John P. Rowan. Chicago: Henry Regnery, 1961.

_____. *Opera omnia*. New York: Musurgia Publishers, 1949. (Photographic reprint of 2d ed., Parma: Petri Fiaccadori, 1852-73).

_____. *Summa theologica*. Biblioteca de Autores Cristianos. Matriti: 1952.

_____. *Summa theologica*. Trans. Fathers of the English Dominican Province. New York: Benziger Bros., 1947.

_____. *Truth, I. Questions i-ix*. Trans. Robert W. Mulligan. Chicago: Henry Regnery, 1952.

Webering, Damascene. *Theory of Demonstration According to William Ockham*. St. Bonaventure, New York: Franciscan Institute, 1953.

Weinberg, Julius R. *Nicolas of Autrecourt*. Princeton: Princeton University Press, 1948.

Wells, Rulon. "Leibniz Today." *Review of Metaphysics*, X (Dec., 1956 and Mar., 1957).

White, Morton G. "The Analytic and Synthetic: an Untenable Dualism." In L. Linksy (ed.), *Semantics and the Philosophy of Language*. Urbana: University of Illinois Press, 1952.

_____. *Toward Reunion in Philosophy*. Cambridge: Harvard Univesity Press, 1956.

Whitehead, A.N. and Bertrand Russell. *Principia Mathematica*. Cambridge: Cambridge University Press, 1964.

William of Ockham. *Summa logicae*. Ed. Philotheus Boehner. St. Bonaventure, New York: Franciscan Institute, 1951.

Wundt, Max. *Die deutsche Schulmetaphysik des 17. Jahrhunderts*. Tübingen: J.C.B. Mohn, 1939.

Yolton, John. *John Locke and the Way of Ideas*. New York: Oxford University Press, 1956.

Yost, R.M. *Leibniz and Philosophical Analysis*. Berkeley: University of California Press, 1954.

For Product Safety Concerns and Information please contact our EU
representative GPSR@taylorandfrancis.com
Taylor & Francis Verlag GmbH, Kaufingerstraße 24, 80331 München, Germany